suspense of a raid from within. This book is an autonomous moment of critical assessment, independent of any final outcome or pre-conceived results.

Peter Swinnen

Brussels (2023)

Luc Tuymans
Christian Kerez
Something Fantastic
Anne Lacaton
Jan De Vylder
Philip Ursprung
Tom Emerson
Laurent Stalder / François Charbonnet
Anri Sala
Maarten Delbeke
Finn Williams
Arno Brandlhuber
ETH Studio Swinnen

Verlag der Buchhandlung Walther und Franz König, Köln

On (Architectural) Abstinence and Obstinacy

This book is a free associative recount of the *I Prefer Not To* lecture series staged between September 2016 and November 2017 at the ETH Department of Architecture (Zurich). Twelve guests touched upon various attitudes of professional abstinence and/or obstinacy. In an offbeat manner, *I Prefer Not To* can be understood as a critical re-assessment of architecture's social and political ethos, often tightly contained and devoid of any unforeseen mischief. Through the words, positions and works of our friends and colleagues *I Prefer Not To* managed – for a brief moment – to install an unformatted stage for problematization and debate.

All twelve stances were eventually entrusted to Youtube, free to pursue eternal public life and varying levels of digital likability. With this publication, we wish to revisit some specific concepts and hidden dimensions of the exposed disquisitions. Each revised lecture is introduced by an editor's note, contextualizing specific choices and unadapted zooms. As an envoi, a conversation with our ETH architecture students is reproduced – a thirteenth ad lib installment offering probes on risk-taking, finding freedoms, proactivity, productive doubt, ghostwriting, the architect as a producer and even boredom as conceivable resources for operating space.

The overarching title of both series and book hints at Herman Melville's prosaic character *Bartleby, the Scrivener* (1853), a subject deemed infamous for his inexplicable social abstinence and intellectual obstinacy. However, we refuse to see Bartleby's auto-inflicted and tortured position as an ideal or pursuable dogma (architecture for that matter already holds enough dogmas). Our particular interest in the position(s) of *I Prefer Not To* is linked to the possibility of a capital pause, the ambiguity of an unsolicited position, the counter-intuitive

Game Changer

The gist of this book reminds me of a mildly radical act by my father, years ago while being a student. He manipulated the assignment cards of the game RISK, creating the option to 'win by eliminating all of your own armies', effectively winning by losing. Despite the numerous disputes we had playing his version with friends, I always liked how this simple creative act questioned the way the game could be played and what goals would be more exciting or meaningful to pursue.

If making architecture would be anywhere close to playing a game, then this book is about thinking and acting beyond a prescribed set of assignment cards. It prefers to push forward an altered game, questioning how one can pursue the more exciting and meaningful goals of architecture. What alternatives can be proposed when refusing to comply with a pre-set brief? Can political agendas and spatial policies be challenged or even changed? And how to critically serve the public good?

These are obviously tricky questions, with many disputable outcomes. Evidently, it is not the first time these questions are posed. Current engaged spatial practices produce all kinds of models, attempting to illustrate what the future practice of architecture could look like and what it should achieve. Certainly, architects often but answer a given brief, though they can equally mediate, initiate, curate, activate, politicize, etc. The ever-widening lens of the architect's capability and accountability offers good reasons for the ongoing critical re-examination of the discipline. Against this backdrop, the lecture series at the ETH Architectural Department and this resultant publication are potential tools for such reconsideration, illustrating and at times questioning the proactive stance of spatial practitioners.

It might be expected that this book aims to persuade a specific model as well, offering appropriate ethical answers and a clear-cut method on how to proceed. However, flipping through these pages offers a different reading. The images do not fill up the architect's reference library, the chapters do not aim to produce a single closed narrative and the content refuses to limit itself to mere architectural topics. A broad variety of positions within the field takes the stage: designer, teacher, student, dean, theoretician and even civil servant. In addition, two artists—Anri Sala and Luc Tuymans—contribute to the generous variety of perspectives.

The diverse contributions are bound together within a tight framework, introduced by the provoking title: 'I Prefer Not To'. As a single given parameter, this overarching credo forces all guest speakers to take a clear position. Even the decision to contribute has to be re-considered. Eventually, what is shown goes far beyond a simple reading of their practice. The selected content reveals how they maneuver and play, both with the given framework and with their respective disciplines. Through layers of reframed information, edits and cuts, this publication does not emphasize a 'good' practice (of architecture); it highlights characters, players and attitudes that might radically redefine or question predefined roles and expectations within their fields.

When diving deeper into the content, some contradicting attitudes can be detected. At times the reader is implicitly urged to let go of ego and authorship as they might stand in the way of serving the public good. On the other hand, it is shown that some characters use fame as a form of leverage to accomplish their proactive goals. Can ego then become a tool to serve the public good? Also, contradicting methods are introduced to challenge predefined directives and rules. Some characters show playful attitudes and find loopholes to subvert existing systems, while others become politicians to change the rules themselves. Can it then so happen that the one might undermine the rules of the other? ...What does it even mean to serve the public good?

No matter how one maneuvers through the field, it is crucial to question what these proactive attitudes should accomplish. What reasons should motivate architects or other spatial practitioners to morph into a teacher, curator, politician, producer, ...? What is the game changer here? Both the answers to these questions as well as an overall position are deliberately left blank. As in all layers of this publication a voluntary sense of stubbornness can be found. With 'I Prefer Not To' as its title, these questions bounce right back to you.

Sophia Holst

Luc Tuymans 13
Christian Kerez 25
Something Fantastic 39
Anne Lacaton 51
Jan De Vylder 57
Philip Ursprung 63
Tom Emerson 77
Laurent Stalder,
François Charbonnet 87
Anri Sala 99
Maarten Delbeke 125
Finn Williams 138
Arno Brandlhuber 153
ETH Studio Swinnen 185
Epilogue 199

It’s How You Lose, (That Matters)

In 1992, just after Jan Hoet's Documenta IX, *two of Charles Saatchi's assistants visited Luc Tuymans at his Antwerp atelier. A brutally 'simple' proposal was brought to the fore: Saatchi wanted to buy an entire year of work for one million euros. Tuymans refused and countered their offer suggesting he could buy one painting every year for the next decade. Soon after the artist received a phone call from Saatchi calling him a 'jackass'. Nothing happened.*

Fast forward, thirteen years later: January 2005, The Triumph of Painting *exhibition (Saatchi Gallery). A high-profile exhibition, entirely devoted to some of the most influential European artists of that moment. By then, Saatchi owned several Tuymans paintings, bought from private collectors. The day after the show's inauguration, all paintings were dumped on the market. Backed by his gallerists, Tuymans bought back the works, making sure they would end up in trustworthy collections. A powerful unsolicited maneuver, reversing the order of art market 'logics'.*

The defining rationale for inviting Luc Tuymans to the lecture series – apart from our mutual appreciation – was particularly provoked by the above story as well as one of his recurring statements: 'I paint and continue to paint because I am not a free man. And of that I am certain'.

PS

Luc Tuymans

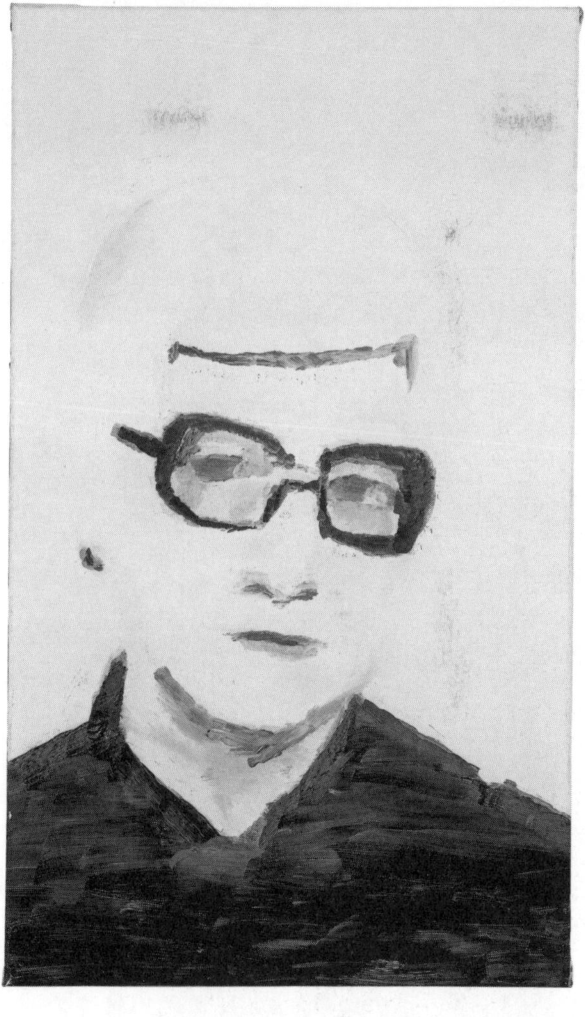

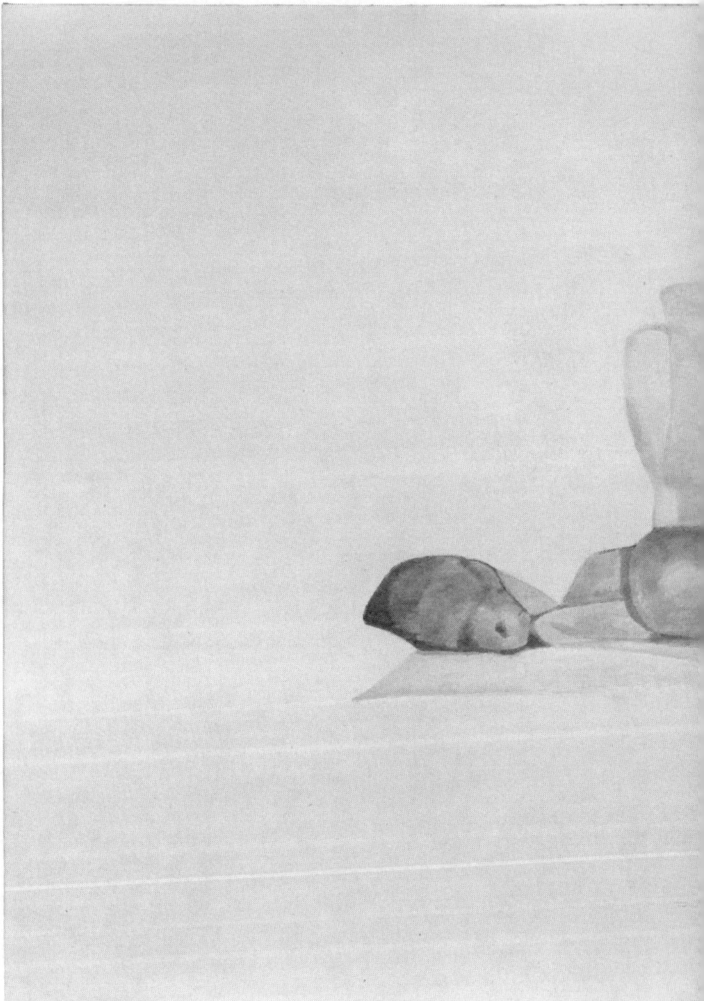

Page 15 Portrait, 2000

Page 17 Maypole, 2000

Page 19 Within, 2001

Page 21 Pigeons, 2001

Page 23 Still Life, 2002

I prefer not to give a lecture.
Thank you very much.

Good... Nobo

~~Lecture~~

I will give a le
showing proje

When I sh
What I will do
in between th
themselves, n
background.

If there's a
I would say it
you constantly
and say what y
you have a clie

There are two versions of this lecture: a disclosed and a non-disclosed one. This binary clearly characterizes Swiss architect Christian Kerez: both an uncoded Einzelgänger *and committed educator.*

For the lecture series we made sure to grant each guest a genuine carte blanche, to the point that we explicitly required not to be informed beforehand on the lecture's nature or content. Five minutes before taking the stage, Christian Kerez took us aside, whispering the lecture's pitch in our ears. The session was to be a dead honest account of his architectural practice so far, so honest that he felt it would be better not to publish the video afterwards. A private lecture of sorts, solely intended for the ETH audience present that night. We nodded and reversed his whisper. Somehow, we expected a different stance, more along the lines of 'I prefer not to give a lecture ...', and then simply walk away. The idea was liked and the 'walkout' got staged accordingly. This became the public YouTube version.

In the non-disclosed reality however, Kerez produced the opposite rendition: offering a truly generous, open and upright testimony on architectural doubts and desires. Though published here in a crossed-out manner – honoring our initial agreement – the lecture's non-disclosed version proves to be all the more cunning and relevant.

PS

Christian Kerez

I prefer not to give a lecture.
Thank you very much.

(applause)

Good... Nobody believes it, what a pity!

(laughter)

I will give a lecture as one gives a lecture as an architect, showing projects. A lecture that is completely affirmative.

When I show the projects, I will not explain them. What I will do is explain the story behind them or the links in between the projects. So not talk about the projects themselves, not defending them, but reflecting on their background.

If there's any connection between architecture and art, I would say it is the art of survival. Because as an architect you constantly have to react. You cannot do the first move and say what you want, how you want it and what it means; you have a client, you have a program, you have a brief, you are invited to competitions and you have to react to that. Of course, you can say 'yes' or 'no', but this is already quite a limited freedom. I somehow believe this is the only freedom you have as an architect, so it is the most interesting question, if you say 'yes' and 'no' and why. I do think saying 'no' doesn't mean anything as such. If you say 'no' to something then ok, what else do you do then, what is the alternative, what is the way out, if you refuse something, if you don't want to accept certain things.

The refusal or the denial becomes a creative act or becomes a productive act. This is what interests me and this is also what I will try to talk about.

AUTOBIOGRAPHY OF DENIAL

~~I conceived this lecture as an autobiography of denial. Because whatever I actually did in my life was never planned. It was never intentional. It was always a reaction to certain things that already were there, trying to always change the situations I found or that were offered.~~

~~I left university and I had to go to work for an office. This was a time when being young was not a quality. It was about having no experience at all and not knowing how things worked. You didn't start with your own office but you started in learning the profession by going to other offices. I wanted to work for Herzog & de Meuron, that at that time had 6 people working for them, yet they didn't take me. I don't know why (laughter).~~

And then I thought, for me they are the best so there's no second best. Then, it doesn't matter where I work. I went to Manpower. This is an institute that gives you a job and you don't have to think for whom you work. I thought it would be interesting to start the profession by finding out what it is about, not as a first step in a career but more as a step to think about: 'Do I really want to do that?' Is architecture as a profession, I mean not as a discipline. As a discipline I thought it was very exciting, but as profession, is it also exciting as a profession? Maybe not, if you look at all the shit which is standing around you and built in our times. So the kind of start was actually to have the almost open experience of the profession. I would say most of what is produced in offices you could describe as building but maybe not as architecture – as a discipline – which has to do with awareness or which has to do with consciousness, which really has a meaning to it.

After one or two years I stopped my profession as an architect and became a photographer. The reason being I thought that the profession is just an obstacle. You have to produce 'the kind of construction drawings' and work on 'a home for elderly people', everything 'out of the catalogue' and doing things 'in the most short possible time', etc. All these things that really matter in professional life. And I thought to survive or to be close to what you love, maybe it is too difficult to do it, but it is maybe not too difficult to look at it and be paid for that, which means becoming a photographer.

I was always fascinated with large buildings and I was always fascinated by the work of engineers, maybe more than architects' works, so I started my conscious life of an architect by photographing engineer buildings, power plants in the mountains. What was fascinating to me was that these constructions were somehow purely conceptual.

There was no thinking about aesthetics, you had to imagine it, it was the eighties and the debate on architecture in

Switzerland was about 'what is the smell of architecture?' Or 'How does it feel if you touch it?' Sensual approaches to the objects of architecture and for me this was totally weird to look at architecture as a pot or a flower. At that time, Herzog & de Meuron just started, Peter Zumthor started, they made all these very small houses, some were blue, some were in wood, they were really beautiful, amazingly beautiful but I was much more fascinated by the big and ugly stuff, that you could also call architecture. And I worked on a book on power plants in the mountains. The way how they look comes out of a necessity. It doesn't come out of any kind of sensual experience or any kind of theory of perception or sensibility but it came out of 'a curve is like this because the pressure of water increases in this way between a topography that looks like this or like that.' So, for me it was also fascinating to look at objects that had a really strong, let's say visual quality, but they were not driven by any desire for visual quality, they were developed by engineers, coming from economical or structural analysis.

Then I worked as an employee in the office of Rudolf Fontana and had the possibility to do the first built project, a chapel in Oberrealta. And it looks like a total contradiction, coming from looking at these huge amazing things just doing a house which is 2 by 5 meters, let's say as big as a table. Most students did much bigger projects, but I would say this chapel is directly related to this experience of looking at buildings in the mountains and also understanding how buildings can change a landscape, how it can change the understanding of a landscape, that is more defined by the relation to the landscape, then it can be looked at as an object for itself. So these are the first things I am going to show you.

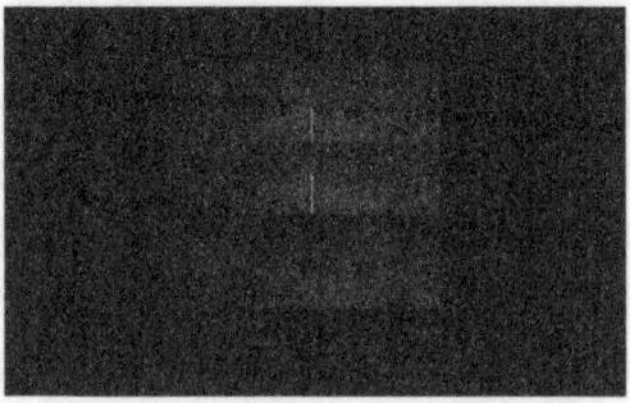

COMPLEXITY

The second chapter is about complexity. After we built the school in Leutschenbach I somehow had the feeling that we had done it already, so no school projects anymore, no local competitions anymore. We go for the large stuff. And I did a series of large projects, unfortunately one of the first we did was the museum in Warsaw, which we won and where I almost went bankrupt, which was perhaps also an interesting experience. Afterwards started to do favela extensions in Brazil and we did some projects in China. I would like to talk about the China experience.

What is the difference between small and large scale? I don't think it has anything to do with dimensions. You can think of a building, which is maybe 200 meters tall, but it is thought of like a small house. You can imagine a house, which always has the same floor plan, which always has the same elements in the façade and then you just repeat it and you multiply elements. But this is somehow not what the large scale offers you. This is actually something you can also accomplish or fulfil, or experience with a small house. I think the repetition becomes then interesting if there's awareness for the differences, that ground floor has different conditions than the top floor, or that in a program brief of 250 000 m² certain areas have a quality which you can never reach in a smaller project. So for me this large scale, or this kind of obsession of the large scale, because if I think of it today I would say probably it is totally unrealistic that

not possible to do something really big and complex, maybe then I could do something really small, and really complex and find the complexity in a totally different scale. When we were asked to do something for the Swiss pavilion at the Venice biennale, we thought this could also be the chance to build something, because at that time I was practically not building anything, except one office building in France, so I thought maybe this is a compensation: it can be built, it can be built in one year, and the kind of madness or strangeness, the complexity that we were looking for, so hard and so long in China, could actually also be found in Switzerland. By the way the pavilion is Swiss grounded so in this sense it is a project in Switzerland even if it is standing in Italy. I don't consider it as a design, I never made any drawing, I also didn't make the model for this project that was built in the end; it was much more trying to push people working on the project over all limits, and coming up with more and more complicated things. Strangely enough, in the end it looked very Chinese.

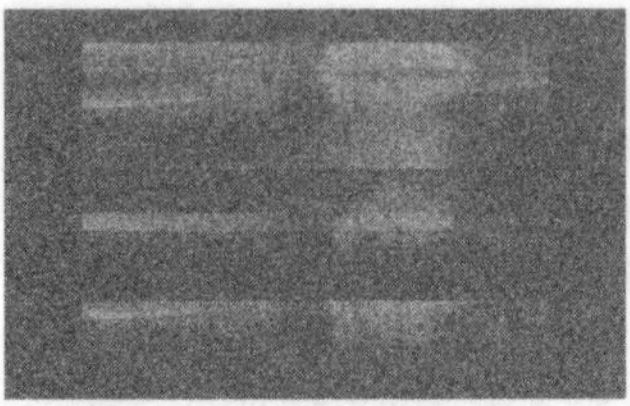

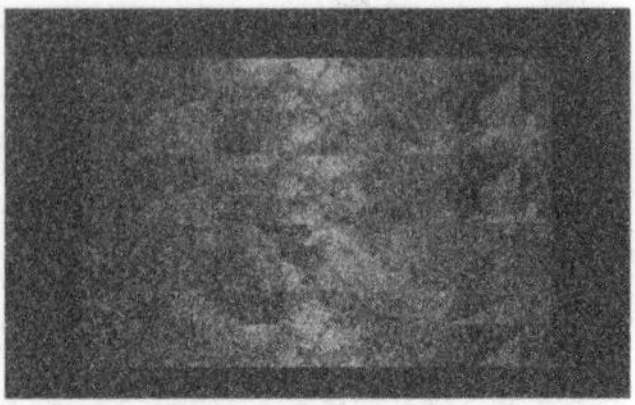

Valerio hates it. I think that's a good sign.

We found a developer from South America who is very interested in buying it.

ENDLESS SPACE

Another detail: One of the challenges that you have as an architect is the client. I basically think in architecture and also at the school we talk a lot about concepts, like an idea is right or wrong. I rather think that a project is driven by a desire. The concept is only the rational trial to communicate that. To work with clients is always very time consuming. It is something – I don't know how it is for other architects – which I think is extremely tiring, it is exhausting. No matter if it is satisfactory, fun or not. But it is such an exhausting work. So I am also constantly thinking of maybe not building anymore private houses. And if I look at all the private houses I built so far, four houses in Switzerland, they are all driven by a desire to create a space which is generous, open, and the concept is very often that you try to avoid the differentiation that you actually have in an apartment. Basically an apartment is just one space and of course it can be divided but the experience of the space is as if it still would be one entire open space.

What is also exciting with this idea or fantasy of a space that is actually nearly the opposite of a private house, is that it is much more about giving up privacy. I don't know exactly where this desire comes from. Maybe just because it is just difficult to achieve, there's still something like South American roots in my work or there's a psychological problem that is the reason for that, I don't know. I also think in the end it doesn't matter, there's no explanation for a desire nor for a concept. And after having worked for several years, I think it was a period of like 6 years, I came to a point where I said I would not accept any private client anymore. And then I got a phone call from a Japanese Czech client that asked me for a private house, a house for himself and two apartments. I wanted to fly to Prague for free since a long time, so I accepted the invitation. And then I realized this client is so different than all the other clients that I know and I also realized that in the end what you design is just the question what you want to design and this is the first and most important and maybe only question. So in this sense if I get tired of private houses it is also maybe just because I do always the same. So

I accepted this client.

This idea of a house that has a lot of spaces and they are very clearly articulated let's say in the parcel way, you can articulate the space which means by a circle, an autonomous form. So this house was built out of autonomous circular spaces and apartments where about 30 % smaller than all the others that I did previously, but the whole house had 5 spaces so it was like an increase of space. I called it autonomous space. I will flip now through these houses probably some you know already, maybe all. But don't be afraid I will not say anything.

CONTEXT

This brings me to the last chapter of my biography and I would like to talk about competitions. I love and hate them. I started entering competitions, losing one after the other. We already lost 25 competitions and then we wondered does it make sense to continue? I heard a story from Jean Nouvel that he did 100 competitions and then he won the first competition. So I thought maybe it is not about entering competitions, winning competitions, maybe it is more about to achieve the '100'. So we went on and the goal was not anymore to win, to not be frustrated, but just to get to the 100.

I think the instrument of competition is extremely delicate. It is not that is as such good or bad, it is something very fragile. I also think democracy is a very good way to rule a country even if somebody like Trump can win an election

I just think it is a sign that every selection process is not as such a clear and safe way to come up with something good. But this doesn't mean that the selection process as such is something you can avoid or is bad but it is just something very fragile and very complex. And I think that competitions should not be looked at who wins and who loses – maybe this is the most boring question in a competition – it is perhaps more exciting if you look at it in the way that different people are working on the same brief, on the same location, in the same time, and are coming to different conclusions. But this means that beside the work inside the jury, there has to be a second work, and this is the reflection, the criticism, and the observation on the work of a jury. This is equally the public debate.

I personally feel that at the moment there is a vanishing of such public debate. It is hard to tell where it comes from and what it means, I personally think it has to do with professionalism, if you show for example after a competition all different entries in a way that each that looks at it can have his own opinion on the jury verdict, which is the basis for a public debate, that this is also dangerous because it can be criticized. So what we experience very often is just the information that is extremely one sided, and avoids debate and public discussion to protect the winning project. This attitude actually doesn't protect the competition process as such but it damages it for this process.

When I started entering competitions, maybe 20 years ago, it was much more about the debate, it was much more about the discussion, to participate in a discussion: ok, you did this and I did that, you have this conviction, I have this one. And it was less important, who was the one in the end who will build it. And today there are also so many competitions, that competitions also as such by nature lost to a certain degree their meaning. And I wonder very much if it is still worth to participate in competitions and I decided for myself to do at least for one year no competition anymore.

~~And not so much because they are very expensive, not so much because of loosing, but just because it is not any more about the debate, I can also do a project just for my self. Without client, without brief, without specific location and it can be even much more exciting. I experience also very often that projects I did they were noticed, they were published, but they were kind of published as a project by Christian Kerez but not as a project for this brief, for this location so they were not in this sense participating in any debate, they were totally isolated.~~

~~I will now show an example of one competition, in which we invested a lot of time. You can look at the competition as a speculation. A competition is also like a race where every body is running in a different direction and then you decide in the end, well this time it was just about economics, next time you decide: well this time it was really about architecture. I hold the opinion, which is totally old fashioned, that these things also can come together. It can happen that you do a competition that is cheaper, faster and better in a conceptual way, in an aesthetic way and so on. So this is one of these projects, which can be measured on any level, etc.~~

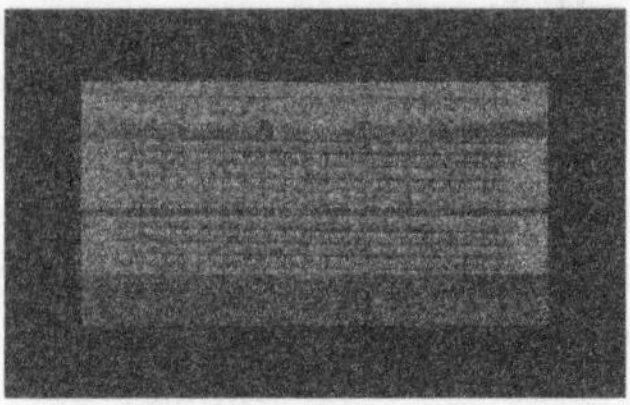

~~The place is called Europa Allee. It was also very much about the question, is there still architecture possible? With all these restriction and constrains. For example El Croquis didn't want to publish it because they say it is so boring. But I thought no, this is exactly the proof that architecture is still possible, even in the centre of Zürich.~~

One of the biggest criticisms on the project was: pigeon shit. The project is not resistant to pigeon shit. We had to get an expertise from an internationally renowned specialist on pigeons and guess what they found out: the building is resistant to pigeon shit. From that moment one, it was no anymore an issue for the jury.

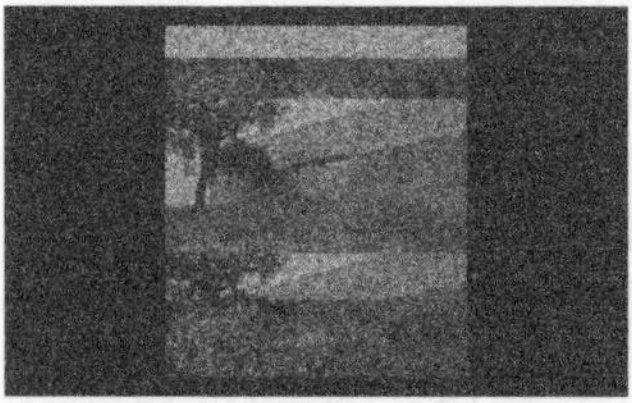

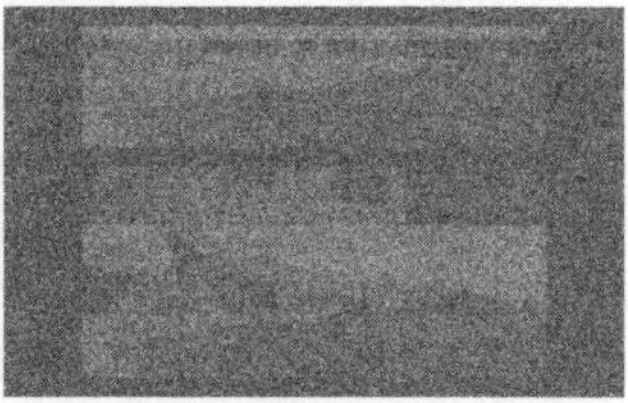

To be honest this last chapter is not closed, I don't have any conclusion what I will do but I just would like to end this lecture with projects of people I admire and of projects I love. I look at this project from Valerio Olgiati also as a political statement. That he took all his time and energy to work for himself. To create a building far away from all possible centres and it is also one of the most beautiful houses I have ever seen. Maybe the other project is less beautiful but I think conceptually, or from the attitude of the architect, from Villa Além to and villa I admire both of these architects for their freedom to say no to something as seductive as competition rituals and to spend all of their time to inventing a location, a brief, an architecture.

Thank you very much.

We want to practice
architecture.

But we prefer not to be sued
for our work, shout into
the phone, work over weekends,
be sho
work a
be unc
just to
becom
money
know a
and wc
materi
togeth
styrofo
fat pro

That s

21 Tickets

Something Fantastic's ethos exudes an intriguing degree of 'I Prefer Not To'. Their principal maxim revolves around finding cracks in the system, transforming unseen potential into a poetic essence and well-being.

Projects devised by Something Fantastic master the art of peripheral conceptualization, perfectly understanding that 'the center need not lie in the middle'. Against this background, inviting them to the lecture series seemed self-evident.

For this volume, I selected their barely legal fashion show at the Neue Nationalgalerie, succinctly evoking Something Fantastic's penchant for détournement. *And for pure intellectual pleasure: have a close look at the ludicrously cheap staging budget (€ 123).*

PS

Something Fantastic

We want to practice
architecture.

But we prefer not to be sued
for our work, shout into
the phone, work over weekends,
be shouted at on the phone,
work at night, lose competitions,
be underpaid, take commissions
just to sustain a big office,
become managers, build with
money from sources we don't
know about, divide between life
and work, work with hazardous
materials, glue everything
together, wrap buildings in
styrofoam, install windows with
fat profiles, design only facades.

That said, we do practice.

These images illustrate a fashion show we 'designed'. Or maybe more fittingly said, refrained from designing. We convinced Perret Schaad, the client, to find the right location for the show rather than to design the right location for the show. The right location seemed to everyone to be Mies van der Rohe's Neue Nationalgalerie. The price to rent it for a day was 50.000 Euros. Perret Schaad did not have 50.000 Euros. We looked up what is allowed in a museum space and what is not. There is no law saying one can't walk a certain choreography in a museum. The open plinth plaza of the Nationalgalerie is a legal grey zone too. Is it public? Is it private? The overhanging roof of the Nationalgalerie seemed to make the risk of rainy weather tolerable. So we risked it. Invited 1000 people to join us at Nationalgalerie via a text message. And bought 23 tickets for the models. The models walked on the inside. The audience watched from the outside. The guards watched too. Cost: 123 Euros, installation and deinstallation time 30 minutes. Waste: a few cigarette butts, one bottle of water, 23 paper tickets. Result: a most appropriate show.

Neue Nationalgalerie by Mies van der Rohe from 1963 and
Perret Schaad Fashion show by Something Fantasitic, 2014

ODD NUMBERS 1,3,5,7,9,11,13,15,17,19,21,23
WALK FIRST LEFT – THEN RIGHT

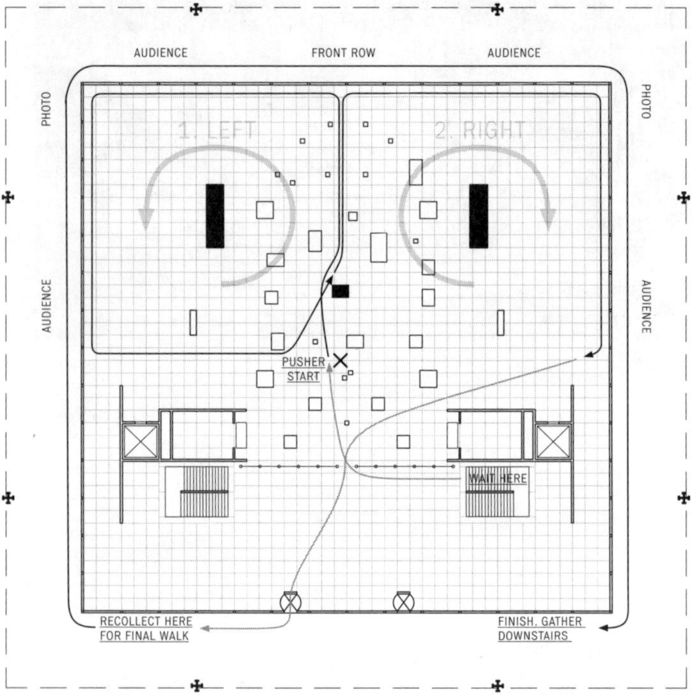

Start: Wait on stairs until you are sent to Pusher.
Walk: -When walking along window: Walk on inner edge of very outer floor tile.
-On central walk towards the front row: walk in the centre of floor tile.
Final Walk: Keep a distance of 3 floor tiles between you. Walk straight, audience will make room for you.
Finish: Meet inside downstairs to go back to changing room together.

Walking Route, Model Group 1

EVEN NUMBERS 2,4,6,8,10,12,14,16,18,20,22,24
WALK FIRST RIGHT – THEN LEFT

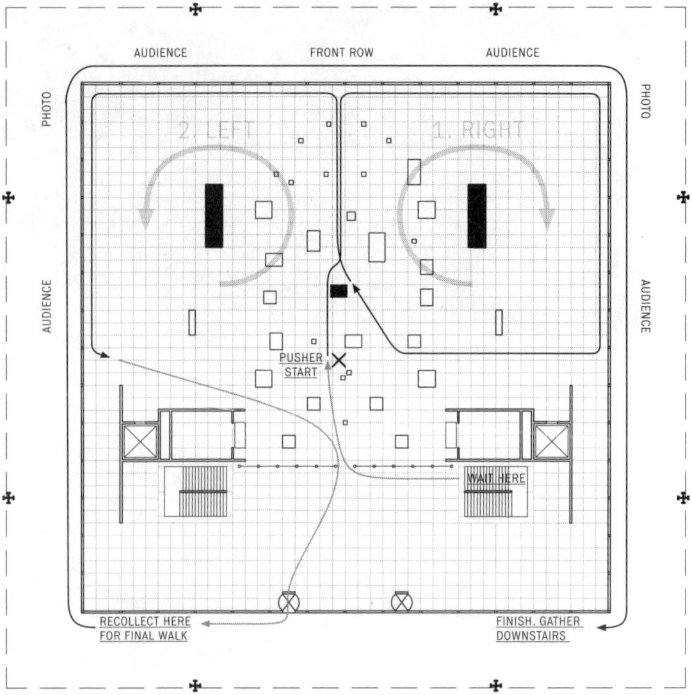

Start: Wait on stairs until you are sent to Pusher.
Walk: -When walking along window: Walk on inner edge of very outer floor tile.
-On central walk towards the front row: walk in the centre of floor tile.
Final Walk: Keep a distance of 3 floor tiles between you. Walk straight, audience will make room for you.
Finish: Meet inside downstairs to go back to changing room together.

Walking Route, Model Group 2

PERRET SCHAAD

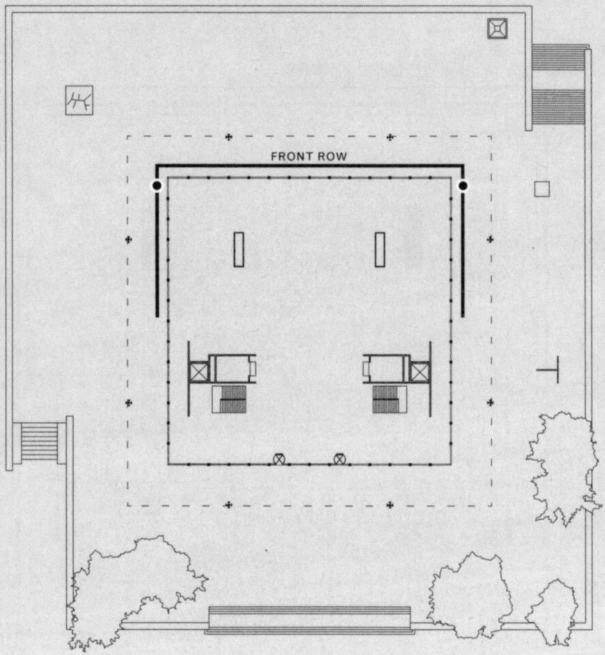

● PLEASE LEAVE THESE SPOTS TO PHOTOGRAPHERS

┏ PLEASE POSITION YOURSELF ALONG THIS LINE FOR BEST VIEW

PLEASE TAKE PICTURES WITHOUT FLASH ONLY

THE NEUE NATIONALGALERIE IS A PUBLIC INSTITUTION AND IN SERVICE DURING THE SHOW.
PLEASE CONSIDER MUSEUM GUESTS AND STAFF.

SPRING SUMMER 2014
MERCEDES-BENZ FASHION WEEK BERLIN

Hand-Out for Guests indicating where to stand

We bought entry tickets for the models ...

The models walked on the inside ...

The audience watched from the outside ...

Neue Nationalgalerie, 30 minutes before the show,
10 minutes into the show and 30 minutes after the show

NOT TO ACCEPT THE MINIMUM

NOT TO UNDERGO THE STANDARD

NOT TO CONSTRAIN

Not to Undergo the Standard

Over the past 25 years I have invited Lacaton & Vassal numerous times to lecture. The very first time was at the Brussels Atomium (of all places), somewhere in the early 2000s. Strikingly, with every consecutive lecture the office's narrative has tightened, skimming off any unnecessary action or narrative. An essential architectural practice finally laid bare.

When inviting Anne Lacaton to the ETH series, we suspected – hoped – that the I Prefer Not To *thematic would be subtly rejected. And so it was. In hardly ninety undisturbed minutes thirty-five years of ethical spatial practice was evidenced. Clear-cut statements on how 'not to demolish', 'not to subtract', 'not to undergo the standard', 'not to lose', ... Counterproposals that have proven to be vital.*

PS

Anne Lacaton

NOT TO
ACCEPT THE
MINIMUM

NOT TO
UNDERGO THE
STANDARD

NOT TO
CONSTRAIN

NOT TO
CUT TREES

NOT TO
ELIMINATE

NOT TO
CLEAR UP

NOT TO
DEMOLISH

NOT TO
SUBSTRACT

NOT TO
LIMIT USES

NOT TO
LOSE

(PROPOSING)
NOT TO DO

55:29 / 1:50:52

43:32 / 1:50:52

1:19:01 / 1:50:52

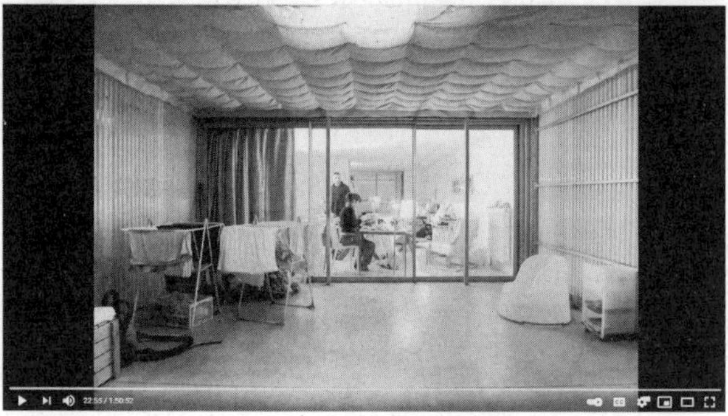
22:55 / 1:50:52

23:27 / 1:50:52

no, no, no, no, no, ...

In 1998 I invited Jan De Vylder for his first-ever lecture. Back then the architecture practice was called IA (NOW)!, *(Instant Architecture Now!). And that is exactly what he and his consecutive partners have been doing ever since: producing fast-paced yet precise architectural interventions, however small the scale, however messy the context. A Belgian pastoral gone galactic.*

Throughout his dense I Prefer Not To *performance one proposal caught the attention. Two plan versions of the same housing project. On the left: the original plan handed in for building approval. On the right: the actual built plan. Noticeably different. During construction the architects discovered new spatial potentials, and decided to execute the project accordingly. Without awaiting official approval. Upon the project's reception, the city's urban administration inspected the site and discovered an entirely different architecture. The authors were forced to re-apply for permission. It would take them over five years to successfully cut the red tape ...*

All in all, this small project holds a key architectural attitude: not to succumb to otherworldly administrative rules but to always perform ad lib, deciding architecture's final design on site.

PS

Jan De Vylder

Original plan handed in for building approval

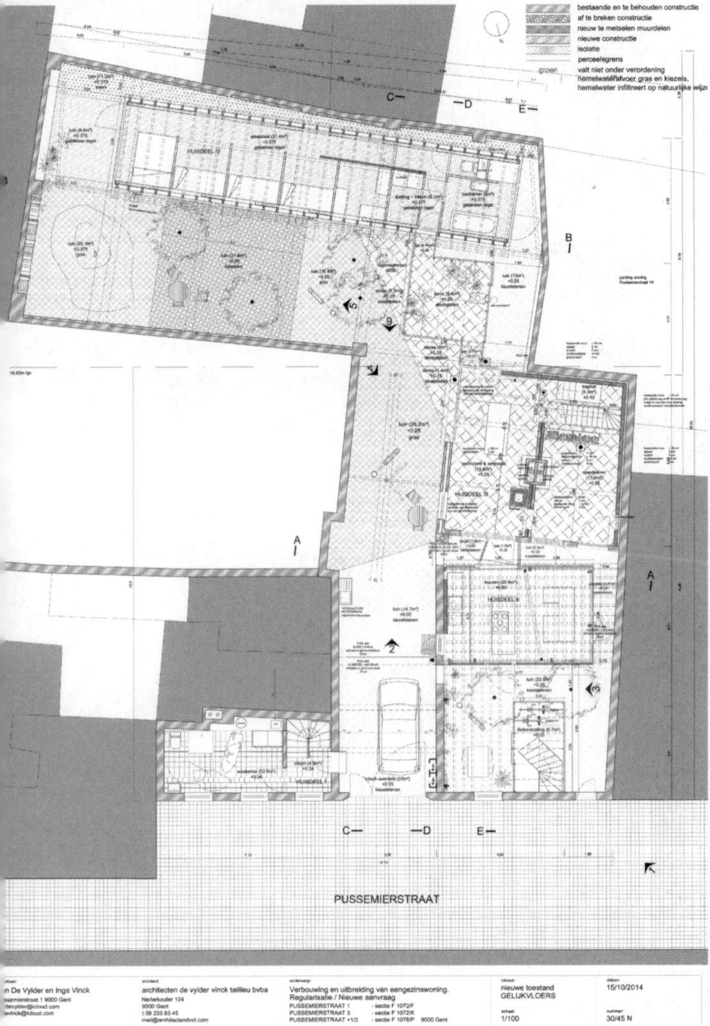

Actual built plan

Architecture – the 'YES' profession par excellence – can deeply and critically learn from the culture of 'NO'. This is the entry point for the series of lectures and I am grateful for the invitation and the possibility to contribute some ideas to the theme and your studio on power. Since the series is about 'no', I will of course challenge the hypothesis of the series, namely that architecture can learn from the culture of no'. I will argue that architecture can learn a lot from the figure of Bartleby. But Bartleby does not say 'no'. He says, 'I prefer not to

Let us first
A Story of Wa
of *Moby Dick,*
November and
The plot can
elderly lawyer
tional scrivene
has two scrive
ceptions and h
sheer quantity
when he first r

'In answer
one morning,
ing open, for i
– pallidly neat
Bartleby.'[2]

Bartleby at
extraordinary
night line, cop
lently, palely,
done by an app
ing something
merely copying
this kind of wo

Bartleby's Room

The I Prefer Not To *lecture series grew organically over three semesters. However, as a stronghold, each season we invited an ETH architectural academic, allowing for an alternative and profound re-reading of the series' mission statement.*

Philip Ursprung is Professor of the History of Art and Architecture and the back then Dean of the Department. Personally, I always was fascinated by his Natural History *dissection of Herzog & de Meuron's work (2002), showcasing a strong capacity for free associative reflection.*

His critical re-visiting of Melville's Bartleby the Scrivener, A Story of Wall-Street *did just that. Especially during the second part of the lecture, introducing the cellular work of Franco-Israeli artist Absalon. For Ursprung these 'rooms' stage a potential imagination for the subjective and internalized space(s) Bartleby had created for himself. Absalon's enclosing work, tensed between withdrawal and (passive) aggression, is indeed a foreseeable example. It only makes one wonder what other specimens could be probed for.*

PS

Philip Ursprung

Architecture – the 'YES' profession par excellence – can deeply and critically learn from the culture of 'NO'. This is the entry point for the series of lectures and I am grateful for the invitation and the possibility to contribute some ideas to the theme and your studio on power. Since the series is about 'no', I will of course challenge the hypothesis of the series, namely that architecture can learn from the 'culture of no'. I will argue that architecture can learn a lot from the figure of Bartleby. But Bartleby does not say 'no'. He says, 'I prefer not to'.

Let us first look at the short story. *Bartleby, the Scrivener: A Story of Wall-Street* written by Herman Melville, author of *Moby Dick*, was first published in *Putnam's Magazine* in November and December 1853, two years after *Moby Dick*.[1] The plot can be resumed as follows: the narrator, a quiet, elderly lawyer with an office on Wall Street employs an additional scrivener, to copy documents for his office. He already has two scriveners, but business is going well with some exceptions and he needs an additional scrivener to handle the sheer quantity of legal documents. He recalls the moment when he first meets Bartleby:

'In answer to my advertisement, a motionless young man one morning, stood upon my office threshold, the door being open, for it was summer. I can see the figure right now – pallidly neat, pitiably respectable, incurably forlorn! It was Bartleby.'[2]

Bartleby at first seems an ideal employee, and 'did an extraordinary quantity of writing. [...] He ran a day and night line, copying by sun-light and by candle-light, [...] silently, palely, mechanically.'[3] His work resembles the work done by an apparatus. It is not creative in the sense of inventing something new and producing something original, but merely copying. The narrator is well aware of the nature of this kind of work: 'I cannot credit that the mettlesome poet

Byron would have contentedly sat down with Bartleby to examine a law document of, say five hundred pages, closely written in a crimpy hand.'[4]

Melville's writings are interesting for architects among other things because of the description of spaces. The spaces in *Bartleby* are less spectacular than those in *Moby Dick*, which consists of 135 chapters filled with the attempts to describe spaces, be it the ocean, the mysterious white whale, the ship, the prosthesis of captain Ahab, etc. But the narrator in *Bartleby* as well gives several accurate descriptions of the room Bartleby works and lives in. It is noteworthy that this room seems very accessible, like in the first episode of Bartleby's appearance on the threshold, the door being open. The narrator describes the organization of the space:

'I should have stated before that ground glass folding-doors divided my premises into two parts, one of which was occupied by my scriveners, the other by myself. According to my humor I threw open these doors, or closed them. I resolved to assign Bartleby a corner by the folding-doors, but on my side of them, so as to have this quiet man within easy call, in case any trifling thing was to be done. I placed his desk close up to a small side-window in that part of the room, a window which originally had afforded a lateral view of certain grimy backyards and bricks, but which, owing to subsequent erections, commanded at present no view at all, though it gave some light. Within three feet of the panes was a wall, and the light came down from far above, between two lofty buildings, as from a very small opening in a dome. Still further to a satisfactory arrangement, I procured a high green folding screen, which might entirely isolate Bartleby from my sight, though not remove him from my voice. And thus, in a manner, privacy and society were conjoined.'[5]

The corner that Bartleby occupies is thus literally an impasse. The earlier view is now blocked, the Wall Street office is facing on the rear another wall. This seems not to bother the scrivener. He makes no mistakes and he is always in the office. He does not even leave the office for lunch like the others, but seems to live solely on cookies that one of the employees delivers to him. However, the routine is interrupted soon. In the words of the narrator:

'It was on the third day, I think, of his being with me [...] that [...] I abruptly called to Bartleby. In my haste and natural expectancy of instant compliance, I sat with my head bent over the original on my desk, and my right hand sideways, and somewhat nervously extended with the copy, so that immediately upon emerging from his retreat, Bartleby might snatch it and proceed to business without the least delay.

In this very attitude did I sit when I called to him, rapidly stating what it was I wanted him to do – namely, to examine a small paper with me. Imagine my surprise, nay, my consternation, when without moving from his privacy, Bartleby in a singularly mild, firm voice, replied, "I prefer not to".'[6]

The 'mild' and 'firm voice' is in contrast to the noise and the movement in the office and outside. The narrator had already been struck by the immobile aspect of his new employee, but now he is confronted with a behavior that he cannot understand. Bartleby's subtle refusal by saying 'I prefer not to' marks the beginning of a tendency that at certain moments makes the reader laugh but that will end tragically. Bartleby first prefers not to work on anything else than the documents assigned to him. After a while he stops writing altogether. He simply sits in his corner, or stands, staring out of the window at the brick wall. The narrator is very patient and empathic. He pities his employee and tolerates his comportment, trying to find an explanation and solution for the mysterious behavior.

One Sunday morning, he makes another surprising discovery. He wants to pick up, on his way to church, something at the office and finds that the door is locked from the inside. Bartleby asks him to come later. When he finally enters, Bartleby has left. The narrator finds out that he lives there:

'Bartleby must have ate, dressed, and slept in my office and that too without plate, mirror, or bed. The cushioned seat of a rickety old sofa in one corner bore the faint impress of a lean, reclining form. Rolled away under his desk, I found a blanket; under an empty grate, a blacking box and brush; on a chair, a tin basin, with soap and a ragged towel; in a newspaper a few crumbs of ginger-nuts and a morsel of cheese.'[7]

In the drawer he finds a handkerchief with savings. But there is no hint about the past of Bartleby, about relations or earlier activities. He tries to dismiss him and give him more money than he owes him, offer him a different job, even send him to Europe, but without success. After a while, his business starts to suffer, clients are irritated by the presence of the scrivener and he eventually moves out of the office. The landlord shows up and complains that Bartleby has still not left and starts living in the staircase after the new tenant has kicked him out of the office. In the end, the landlord calls the police to imprison him as vagrant. The narrator visits him in the infamous Tombs of New York in a grim building in Egyptian style, and provides him with money, but Bartleby prefers not to eat.

The lawyer's office, the place where Bartleby works and lives resembles to some extent a prison cell. The narrator does not reflect this – for him it looks open – but he has pity for the loneliness of Bartleby and even offers him to come and stay at his own house. In contrast to the office, the prison is described as an open space. Bartleby is free to move where he wants, and he even has access to a courtyard that is not accessible to normal prisoners. This is where he will die.

'The yard was entirely quiet. It was not accessible to the common prisoners. The surrounding walls, of amazing thickness, kept off all sounds behind them. The Egyptian character of the masonry weighed upon me with its gloom. But a soft imprisoned turf grew under foot. The heart of the eternal pyramids, it seemed, wherein, by some strange magic, through the clefts, grass-seed, dropped by birds, had sprung.'[8]

The narrator ends the story by telling the reader that he shortly after his death heard a rumor that Bartleby had been 'a subordinate clerk in the Dead Letter office at Washington, from which he had been suddenly removed by a change in the administration. [...] Dead letters! does it not sound like dead men? Conceive a man by nature and misfortune prone to a pallid hopelessness, can any business seem more fitted to heighten it than that of continually handling these dead letters, and assorting them for the flames?'[9] And the story ends: 'Ah Bartleby! Ah humanity!'[10]

How can we interpret the short story? Many options are plausible, for instance the idea that Bartleby is suffering a depression and that his unwillingness to work is a symptom for this disease long before it could be diagnosed. Giorgio Agamben, in his text 'Bartleby, or, on Contingency' gives another interpretation.[11] Agamben does not interpret Bartleby's reaction as 'no', but as the plea for the potential. 'I prefer not to', this unfinished sentence, remains halfway between yes and no. It is interesting and attracting precisely because it does not decide and keeps the potential open. For Agamben, Bartleby is a symbol for skepticism, the mistrust of any certainty and therefore a model for critical thinking.

Agamben's text was published in the early 1990s. Today, I would give another interpretation. In the novel, the characters are entirely defined by their work, by their performance. Bartleby at first seems to be the ideal worker. Work and life blend entirely, he is always available and asks for nothing except a minimum of space and food. But the obsolescence of the human workforce is already inscribed into the narration by Melville. What the scriveners are doing, we as readers know today, could be done by a machine. When Bartleby stops working, he cannot be reached anymore. The compassion that the narrator has is, I think, a result of him seeing his own mirror image in Bartleby. One day, he will not be able to work, and perhaps not be able to leave his room. Bartleby thus becomes the symbol of the biggest fear of the subject in a capitalist society, namely the absence of work - unemployment. He embodies both the presence and the absence of work. He embodies the ideal of the modern worker as someone who is restless, fully identified with his labor and self-exploiting. And he embodies the contrary, namely the worker who cannot work or who refuses to work because of a strike.

If we look back at the novel from the perspective of today, Bartleby seems to prefigure a subject who can choose among various activities, yet who is also made responsible for this choice. The book *The Weariness of the Self* by the sociologist Alain Ehrenberg offers a viable link between the history of depression, culture, and economy. The author sheds light on the linkage of depression and the twin poles of a globalized economy and unemployment, on the one hand, and exhaustion through over-work on the other. Essentially, what interests Ehrenberg is how individuals are over-strained by the demands their environment places on them, both in the form of real pressure and through the internalization of competition. He states that 'the depressed individual [...] is tired of having to become himself.'[12]

How can we imagine the spaces of these subjects? What would be a room for Bartleby, today? In the domain of architecture as such, I cannot give an answer. But if we turn our attention towards art, or towards art forms close to architecture, we inevitably come to the artist Absalon (1964-1993).[13] Absalon's oeuvre, I would argue, stakes out the terrain on which depression arises by expressing the tensions to which people are exposed by their own standards and those of their environment. A recurrent theme in his art works is the mixture of withdrawal and aggression, impotence and anger, activity and passivity, isolation and extroversion, all of which are characteristic of depressive complaints. In the video-recorded performances *Solutions* (1992) for instance, the performer moves in office garb undecidedly between stylized furniture pieces in a narrow, white interior. He pours himself a drink at the desk, lies down on a bunk bed, takes a bath, stands in a corner. The actor offers 'solutions' for countless requirements. But the mixture of freedom and confinement and the stereotyped actions are reminiscent of Ehrenberg's observation that individuals become over-strained if they have to make all the choices and decisions themselves. In Ehrenberg's words: 'We are changing, of course, but that does not necessarily mean we are progressing.'[14]

The projects and models developed in the late 1980s culminate from 1992 onwards in the *Cellules*, small provisional lodgings made of wood to be inhabited by the artist and destined for Paris, Zurich, New York, Tel Aviv, Frankfurt and Tokyo. Unlike earlier works, the *Cellules*, which Absalon also called houses ('maison') are not conceived as a utopia, but as functioning accommodation. They are essentially something that would today be called an 'intervention', that would thus spur a 'densification' of his own life, as Absalon puts it and combine this with its public impact.[15] Indeed, while the inside is tailored to the artist's needs, providing space for two pairs of pants and shirts and a maximum of 15 books, it has a pipe connection for water and sockets for power and phone lines, the outside responds to the specifics of the urban location. The *Cellule* planned for Paris also interested Absalon because in the eyes of the public authorities it constituted neither a sculpture nor architecture and therefore, in his opinion, required the introduction of a new law in order for him to be able to erect it outdoors. The cell designed for Zurich was 'the least sentimental house, the "coldest"'.[16] And the one he created for Frankfurt looks like a cross between a 'watchtower and a bunker'.[17]

Absalon accepted the imperative that every person is responsible for him- or herself. Within the confines of the art world (but visible beyond) he acted the way the globalized economy wants its subjects to be, i.e. mobile, autonomous,

Absalon, Cell No. 4 (prototype), 1992

independent, always under just so much strain. And at the same time he held a mirror up to the world. Because the segmentation and individualization impacts on the coherency of urban life, where the *Cellules* threaten to attack the smooth mechanisms of the industrial nations like a 'virus', as Absalon put it.[18] The *Cellules* cannot simply be multiplied, each is unique. They are anything but perfect and instead fragile and subject to wear and tear. They require constant improvement and repair. Just as depression, which society has decided is a tolerable price to pay for itself, threatens to interrupt the smoothly expanding economy, so the *Cellules* potentially halt the dynamics of the city. They are monuments to particularization.

The lecture series suggest that we can learn from the 'no' of Bartleby. It puts autonomy at the core of the discipline, the heroic 'no' being an ideal that stands for the freedom of architecture as a discipline. I personally have difficulties to enumerate cases, where architects said 'I prefer not to'. I remember Peter Zumthor being invited for a skyscraper in Korea and declining the offer. But usually it is 'yes'. Even for an utterly absurd project to build a 400 meter high tower hotel in the Swiss mountain village of Vals where wealthy tourists should be flown in by helicopter, many famous international architects participated in the competition and the jury. But this is certainly due to the fact that architecture is a 'culture of yes'. Perhaps today's role models are mainly those of the architect as pragmatic and opportunistic. Architects seem to be content to solve the problems posed by others, be it politicians, developers, or clients. I think the heroic 'no' is not the adequate answer because it leads towards polarity. 'Yes' and 'no' are a kind of mirror images of each other. I am very favorable, however, towards the idea of the architect who is skeptical both towards architecture and towards politics. This attitude is fruitful and open to change. 'I prefer not to' means that one does not identify with, say, the client or the user of the building. And it is close to 'I prefer.'

1 Herman Melville, "Bartleby, the Scrivener. A Story of Wall-street," in *Putnam's Monthly: A Magazine of Literature, Science, and Art*, New York, Vol. II, November 1853, No. XI, p. 546-557; Conclud ed Vol. II - December 1853, No. XII, p. 609-615, Online-Edition Bartleby.com, 1999, pages indicated according to the online edition 1999, accessed November, 2018.
2 Ibid., p. 15.
3 Ibid., p. 18.
4 Ibid., p. 19.
5 Ibid., p. 17.
6 Ibid., p. 20-21.
7 Ibid., p. 88.
8 Ibid., p. 244.
9 Ibid., p. 250.
10 Ibid., p. 251.
11 See Giorgio Agamben, "Bartleby, or, on Contingency," in Giorgo Agamben, *Potentialities, Collected Essays in Philosophy*, (Stanford: Stanford University Press, 1999), p. 243-274.
12 Alan Ehrenberg, *The Weariness of the Self, Diagnosing the History of Depression in the Contemporary Age*, (Montreal & Kingston: McGill-Queen's University Press, 2010), p. 4.
13 See my essay 'Design of the In/human: *Absalon* and the spaces of depression', in *Absalon*, ed. by Susanne Pfeffer, KW Institute for Contemporary Art Berlin, (Cologne: Verlag der Buchhandlung Walther König, 2011), p. 273-285.
14 Ehrenberg, 2010, p. 185.
15 'Ces maisons vont conditionner ma vie, toujours dans ce désir [...] de le densifier, de le rendre plus juste, plus précis,' Absalon, lecture, Ecole Nationale Supérieure des Beaux-Arts, Paris (May 4, 1993); transcribed by Cédric Venail, unpublished manuscript, translation of the quote by author.
16 'C'est la maison la moins sentimentale, la plus froide à mes yeux, et c'est tout à fait mon sentiment par rapport à cet endroit', ibid.
17 Ibid.
18 Ibid.

The prism through which I am going to do this talk is not Anglo-Saxon, it's neither English nor American, it's actually French, and the title *I Prefer Not To* is quite problematic and I think that is specifically, I guess that is deliberately why Peter choose it because it it puts us all off base. It is not the way we are used to behaving, it is not the way we are used to behaving in relation to institutions, or commissions or clients. We are trained to say yes. So I found it very difficult to try and think about the notions of when I said no and what

were the motiv
in the title *I Pr*
has this kind o
judgment to it.
student in Can
on this guy he
the sixties and
ary group – th
but particularl
the letter 'e' c
he is particula
work. And thi
it is a little bit
texts, a fairly u
Prefer Not To r
in 1981, so ve
most importa
Imagining an I
of text, poem,

I wouldn't
but somet

I'd love to
but somet

On the Difficulty of
Imagining an Ideal City
(reprise)

Just before entering the ETH lecture hall, Tom Emerson 'warned' me that it was going to be a very (!) short talk. A mere 10 minutes. Georges Perec's text On the Difficulty of Imagining an Ideal City *(1981) was to serve as a primer. A highly personal elegy on 'preferring' followed. A thoroughbred architectural short track.*

PS

Tom Emerson

The prism through which I am going to do this talk is not Anglo-Saxon, it's neither English nor American, it's actually French, and the title *I Prefer Not To* is quite problematic and I think that is specifically, I guess that is deliberately why Peter choose it because it it puts us all off base. It is not the way we are used to behaving, it is not the way we are used to behaving in relation to institutions, or commissions or clients. We are trained to say yes. So I found it very difficult to try and think about the notions of when I said no and what were the motivations for it. So I slightly shifted the emphasis in the title *I Prefer Not To* towards the 'prefer', because that has this kind of ambiguous element to it, it has an element of judgment to it. And ever since I was a student, when I was a student in Cambridge for my diploma, I wrote a dissertation on this guy here. Georges Perec. A great French writer from the sixties and seventies who is part of an experimental literary group – the Oulipo – and he wrote just about everything but particularly with constraints. He wrote a novel without the letter 'e' called *La disparition* or *A void* in English. But he is particularly interesting in the treatment of space in his work. And this is not a talk about Georges Perec, although it is a little bit at the beginning, it is really taking one of his texts, a fairly unknown one, as the starting point. The title *I Prefer Not To* reminded me a little bit of a text he published in 1981, so very late in his career, after he had written his most important books, and it's called *On the Difficulty of Imagining an Ideal City*. And I am going to read it. It is a sort of text, poem, or whatever.

> I wouldn't like to live in America
> *but sometimes I would*
>
> I'd love to live on the Boulevard St. Germain
> *but sometimes I wouldn't*

I wouldn't like to live on a coral reef
but sometimes I would

I wouldn't like to live in a dungeon
but sometimes I would

I wouldn't like to live in the East
but sometimes I would

I love living in France
but sometimes I don't

I'd love to live in Greenland
but not for too long

I'd like to live to a hundred
but sometimes I wouldn't

(it's sad though he died at 46)

I wouldn't like to live in Issoudun
but sometimes I would

I wouldn't like to live on a junk
but sometimes I would

I wouldn't like to live in a ksar
but sometimes I would

I'd have loved to go in a lunar module
but it's a bit late

I wouldn't like to live in a monastery
but sometimes I would

I wouldn't like to live at the Hôtel Negresco
but sometimes I would

I wouldn't like to live in the open air
but sometimes I would

I love living in Paris
but sometimes I don't

I wouldn't like to live in Quebec
but sometimes I would

I wouldn't like to live by my own resources
but sometimes I would

I wouldn't like to live in a submarine
but sometimes I would

I wouldn't like to live in a tower
but sometimes I would

I wouldn't like to live with Ursula Andress
but sometimes I would

I wouldn't like to live in a village
but sometimes I would

I wouldn't like to live in a wigwam
but sometimes I would

I'd love to live in Xanadu
but not for ever

I wouldn't like to live in the Yonne
but sometimes I would

I wouldn't like us all to live in Zanzibar
but sometimes I would

I've always kind of liked this piece and in fact when I wrote my dissertation I never mentioned it because I never really knew what he meant. Even though I found it quite moving, quite insightful and at the same time sort of throwaway and kind of playful without any additional meaning. So what I have done is that I have done my own version, but I prefer not to. So this is going to be a very short talk. And I suppose this is my own take on *I Prefer Not To*.

I like being an architect
but sometimes I'd rather be the artist
Or even, an author

I would love growing up in Belgium in the 1970s
with Jacques Brel playing in the background
but I prefer not to live that forever

I appreciate the importance of classicism
but I prefer simple carpentry

I love the idea of dancing
but I would prefer not to

I prefer excavations
You can discover nearly everything

Finishing things is important
but sometimes I would prefer not to

This garden in Rome is my favourite
architectural drawing

I like the idea of a helping hand
but sometimes I prefer not to

And who wouldn't prefer to live in Italy?

I prefer the way things are repaired in Japan

And Tom Sachs said that you should always be knolling
and I prefer that

I do prefer knolling

I love living in London
but sometimes I prefer to live in Los Angeles

I often prefer making things to drawing them

I prefer cities at night
but not always

Today, second year students are planting an oak tree
For that I would prefer to be outside with them

I would prefer not to live in the past
but it is not always easy

A quoin is a well-dressed stone that turns the corner
but I prefer quoins that are underdressed

I would love to be Robinson Crusoe
but I would miss too many people

Space is overused in architectural conversations
and I prefer not to

To Have and Have Not is my favourite film
but I prefer not to watch it everyday

I prefer not to believe in utopia

I am ashamed to say that I have never read Vitruvius
and I would prefer not to

I know that water is the source of all life
but some things I prefer not to

There are so few words beginning in X
but I prefer not to

I prefer a yard to a meter
but a meter is more useful

Sometimes I'd like it for all of us to live in Zurich
but sometimes I prefer to get away

Electronic Letters (on Bartleby)

Dear François,

Your idea about preparing our talk by email helps me to overcome my initial 'no' to participating in Peter's lecture series. Indeed, while thinking on how to engage with the topic, there seemed to me to be only two options: a personal account about one's work or about situations where one failed or succeeded to say 'no', or a theoretical account about refusa
issue in human relat
the possibility of failu
me: hence, my doub
Peter's question.

Of course, in the firs
tried to tell entertaini
not becoming entert
as nobody has time
seriously with archite
with architectural his
the public laugh in re
failures and success
always entertaining
of teachers. We kno
school years. But wh
from that? – certainl
'no'. And above all, s
seems to me inappro
make an autobiogra

In the second case,
the sheer difficulty o
embarrassed me. O
take an intelligent an
Scrivener' and make
have the ambition to
takes quite a while.
literature, you have t
and you have to writ
the end, nobody und
your text is too elabo

That said, how shall
discover while writin
account, there are p
a verbal expression;
immensity of a topic
fear of failure; and a
doubt in avoiding en

Your proposal to switch the topic slightly from 'no' to 'doubt' is one of those shifts for which you are a champion, and I think to illustrate it with *Caravaggio's Incredulity of St Thomas* would have been a perfect way to illustrate 'doubt'. We could have done a close analysis, as you suggested, about the gaze of Thomas or about the light, the movement of the bodies, etc. But Peter refused. He is better than we are at

*Inviting Laurent Stalder, Professor of Architectural Theory and Director of the Institute for the History and Theory of Architecture (ETH), was not an easy operation. The first two invitations to lecture were simply declined. In the end a sparring partner was proposed: Stalder's long-time 'partner-in-architecture' François Charbonnet (*Made in Sàrl*). Their mutual endeavor was crystallized through an intense e-mail communication brushing a wide variety of* I Prefer Not To *assumptions. The tool offered by 'electronic messages' enabled to refrain from any pre-given outcome or final position. During the performance, Stalder and Charbonnet read each other's prose. A potential script for an intriguing exchange about the concept of NO-thing.*

PS

Laurent Stalder, François Charbonnet

Dear François,

Your idea about preparing our talk by email helps me to overcome my initial 'no' to participating in Peter's lecture series. Indeed, while thinking on how to engage with the topic, there seemed to me to be only two options: a personal account about one's work or about situations where one failed or succeeded to say 'no', or a theoretical account about refusal – denial as a key issue in human relations. In both situations, the possibility of failure seemed very high to me: hence, my doubts about engaging with Peter's question.

Of course, in the first case, one could have tried to tell entertaining stories – and are we not becoming entertainers more and more, as nobody has time and leisure to engage seriously with architecture and, even more, with architectural history? – and to make the public laugh in recalling situations about failures and successes in saying 'no'. It is always entertaining to hear about the failures of teachers. We know it all too well from our school years. But what would we really learn from that? – certainly, nothing about saying 'no'. And above all, speaking about myself seems to me inappropriate. I am not here to make an autobiography.

In the second case, probably, it was the sheer difficulty of the task which embarrassed me. Of course, one could just take an intelligent analysis of 'Bartleby, the Scrivener' and make a resume. But if you have the ambition to write your own story, it takes quite a while. You have to find the right literature, you have to clarify your position, and you have to write an ambitious text. In the end, nobody understands you because your text is too elaborated.

That said, how shall we proceed? As I discover while writing, already in this short account, there are plenty of 'noes'. 'No', as a verbal expression; 'no' in response to the immensity of a topic; a 'no' which hides the fear of failure; and a 'no' which deals with doubt in avoiding engagement.

Your proposal to switch the topic slightly from 'no' to 'doubt' is one of those shifts for which you are a champion, and I think to illustrate it with *Caravaggio's Incredulity of St Thomas* would have been a perfect way to illustrate 'doubt'. We could have done a close analysis, as you suggested, about the gaze of Thomas or about the light, the movement of the bodies, etc. But Peter refused. He is better than we are at saying 'no'.

As I am writing this, I also begin to doubt your proposal. As always, the shifts you suggest open up the situation, stimulate. But is 'doubt' not something other than a 'refusal', than saying 'no'?

I do not know yet if this journey will lead somewhere.

Looking forwards to hearing from you,

Laurent

Dear friend,

Let me in the first place thank you for your initial message which unveils a slightly erratic stance towards the suggested issue; and ironically enough, you seem to literally embody the locution '*I'd prefer not to*'. As a first statement, whether conscious or unconscious, I find that quite joyful; we could stop right where your mail comes to an end...

I share your protestant point of view regarding the opportunity to speak about oneself... after all, the reasons for refusal are often too intimate to be shared, and it could be a deleterious – but very contemporary – shift towards self-exhibition: let's not speak about us... although as you said, we'd probably face a very complacent public on the matter, and vanity would most certainly become the marker of our singularities. Not very promising.

Hence my proposal, as you rightly grasped, to opportunistically deflect an all-too-assertive reading of Bartleby's leitmotiv and to question the nature of doubt, once said that the cultivation of it is, I believe, central to any innovative thinking. But of course, I understand your reaction towards my proposal to debate about *The Incredulity of St Thomas*, and you are definitely right when you distinguish doubt and refusal... but wouldn't you agree that doubt is often the reason for legitimate *refusal*? In other words, isn't doubt one of the secret agents of *defiance*?

Yet our host Peter feels otherwise, and as I respect any critical mind, let us try to at least outline a series of positions, based on subjective readings of Melville's short story. And for once, we are not asked to talk about what one has done – which implicitly suggests a justification process – but about what one has refused to do, to say or to advise. The question literally seems to be about NO-THING, but how does one speak about nothingness? Wouldn't a physicist be more appropriate? I mention the physicist not to evade our responsibility but because I don't think that the scientist is really interested in nothingness, but rather in the consequences of such a conceptual intendment... so my question is: should we discourse about refusals or about the consequences of defiance? It isn't obvious to me, yet.

P.S. before we engage in a kind of uncertain – but promising – dialogue, I would like to share with you this brief essay by Gilles Deleuze; as often with him, 'Bartleby; or, the Formula' is a luminous speculation that travels at great speed and surely will enlighten the object of our correspondence.

To be continued.

My warmest thoughts to the whole family.

François

Dear Laurent,

I have just read Melville's story... and was quite shaken by it! Shall we start debating? ... Comments on 'Bartleby' often qualify its main character as an epitome of *resistance*, but I personally have a slight problem with such a reading: isn't resistance always *active* or *re-active*? I of course know that common language accepts the idea of a passive resistance, but a *will* is always what allows it to be triggered... and to me Bartleby seems to be candidly devoid of any *will*; even his leitmotiv-formula isn't really a NO, but a softened version of it: that can't just be politeness! It is the attribute of a personality without any asperity, which therefore doesn't cast any shadow as a hint of his flesh.

Bartleby indeed writes and works and up to a certain extent also performs the task he's been hired for; but the *temperature* of his resolution constantly drops, reaching what thermodynamics would call *absolute zero*: the temperature at which nothing, not even the smallest particle, remains in motion: -273.15°C... Bartleby must be one of the coldest and most absolute voids literature has ever produced; and in order to make that most obvious, Melville loads the story with sharply characterised *electrons*, whose agitation and madness increase in inverse proportion to the condition of Bartleby's will. The contrast is stunning! But you most certainly know that *absolute zero* is actually a projection! It can in fact never be reached... The projection – or prophecy – can therefore never be fully accomplished, which echoes a certain idea of the architectural project and its corollary attributes, namely:

- A1. An impulse (where kinetic energy is at its highest: the earliest stage of the project...- ile!)
- A2. In the course of development, this kinetic energy is transformed into a potential energy
- A3. A speed, as a function of time (m/s)
- B. A trajectory which would come from the stand taken in a given problematic
- C. A moving target
- D. Deflective actions to adjust with the constantly evolving position of the target

Considered in such a prospect, a project can hardly be stifled by a definitive state: it is in essence dynamic. And Bartleby becomes the fixed axis around which the fleeting and futile trajectories of capitalistic lives revolve.

I personally see no equivalent to Bartleby... certainly not in the field of architecture. Deleuze, in his essay, qualifies him as the ultimate *Original*; but is he an origin or an end? And what is an origin? Isn't the *concept of origin* a modern one?

Amitiés, François

Dear François,

Thank you for your *projectile-reading* of 'Bartleby', which is indeed a very convincing one; it also leads to death, therefore to an end and might therefore be understood as a failed project.

But maybe there is another dimension, a less architectural one, less embedded in an isolated reading of the *projectile*/Bartleby. This reading might have less to do with one subject, but between different ones or between a subject and his milieu. Bartleby does not act but stays in place, is erratic and contaminates his surroundings. By being erratic in a moving world, with different modes, he claims his subjectivity, while the others, considered at first glance more individual, become more and more passive.

This is a short note while waiting for the plane, where this static-dynamic relation is at its highest.

All my best,
Laurent

Dear friend,

I very much agree with your statement and alternative reading; and I believe that the phenomenon you describe can be applied to any meaningful outlandishness – to use Melville's formula – in other words, peculiar behaviour or idiosyncrasies.

And I would even be tempted to propose a scientific flipside analogy: couldn't Bartleby's behaviour be that of a *black hole*, a supreme attraction force that swallows its surroundings and precipitates behavioural disruptions on the part of the other characters? The only course of action left to the human satellites revolving around him would therefore be a constrained estrangement... Bartleby's essence is viral and the effect of his behaviour can only lead to the most improbable astonishment; it is literally *un-believable*, that is it exceeds all comprehensive dimensions and triggers as a result a vortex of erratic conducts.

But I don't think that Bartleby stands alone in this state; one has to recall Hector Berlioz's reaction to his first hearing of Beethoven's fifth symphony, leaving the concert hall in a state of frenzy and hysteria: the work had reached beyond what one could decently apprehend, ultimately setting a fixed and irreducible moment in the history of music: *to give birth to such singularity is threatening!* – as the revolutionary French composer suggested. And cultural history is full of such moments leading to most sinister or most glorious consequences (from Galileo to Stravinsky and his *Rite of Spring*, through Beethoven and Kafka): the sudden eruption of the unknown and therefore of the *inconceivable*. In a word, 'preposterous' stands for that which radically inflects one's way of capturing reality!

Amitiés, François

Dear François,

I have been thinking on how to read your email. It seems contradictory in its formulation. On the one side, echoing Deleuze's idea of projectile (is it from *Le Pli. Leibniz et le Baroque*?), it proposes a positive reading of the 'I would prefer not to', a radical trajectory towards a goal that can never be reached, which, on the other side, seems completely at odds with Bartleby's fate, as his refusal brings him to his own end.

While I was searching for an issue out of this contradictory situation, I found this video of Giacometti from 1962, which could help us take a step further, as Giacometti proposes a reading of his work as a permanent refusal of the convention of artistic or more general visual practice, of secured meaning, but at the same time as the pursuit of a goal, to better understand what he sees. Could this be a trajectory out of the desperation of Bartleby?

All my best,
Laurent

Dear Laurent,

My digression or deflection of Bartleby's behaviour is contradictory only for the reason, I believe, that Bartleby is a literary character and that his trajectory can only tip either on one side – *life* – or on the other – death: but this *either/or* dichotomy only applies to a living subject; what of an inert object or of an idea, as in the case of architecture? None of them have to choose – and in fact they can't! – but they can latently remain an ever-lasting potential with indefinite borders... which takes us to Giacometti's statements, as he sees his work as a constantly evolving and never accomplished one; it is embedded in a perpetual movement of approach without being able – or even wishing – to reach its final state. It is as if Giacometti had raised the status of the *repentir* – which shows the essential uncertainty of overlaid preliminary drafts – to the final level of representation, refusing to give its work a categorical outline: the doubt not expressed as a *state of mind*, but as a *state of the art*! It is an *Auseinandersetzung* with time, and a wide part of Giacometti's corpus oscillates between static and dynamic figures, each one acquiring characteristics of the other: a vibrating head or a stifled walking silhouette: contradictions in terms!

I personally see the architectural project in a similar way: it has to be kept on the move of a fleeting trajectory, and as such, time becomes of course one of its most influential parameters.

You see, I think one should deny the death of Bartleby – *the character* – the right to bring the velocity of an idea to an end: I simply think that death is in this case a literary feature, and had the story for any reason gone on, the revolving characters around him might well have used all their respective energies to a final state of nothingness, used and abused by the forces of friction that Bartleby's vortex created around them. To be continued.

Amitiés,
François

Dear François,

This short note is to thank you, much too late, for your Deleuzian text.

It seems that here again our two approaches to problems show up in all their clarity: on the one side your systematic way of analysing a problem in framing its general issues and on the other my empirical one by collecting examples.

Here some other 'noes': the *Nein-Sager*: a conservative person who does not want to change the existing world as it is considered perfect, the *Nein-Sager* of Berthold Brecht. The story is of a boy who is not ready to sacrifice himself for his community; the 'no' of the 'terrible twos', the age in which children begin to make their own choices by opposing every possible thing/remark/decision with a 'no'. This 'no' seems to relate to the construction of one's own identity. There would be plenty of other examples: the German substantive—*no-go*, an Anglicism from the noun 'no-go'. It means an interdiction or a taboo. Further: 'non-stop', 'no way'.

There are many different ways of saying 'no'. As soon as I have read 'Bartleby', I will get back to you.

All my best, Laurent

Dear François,

I just finished 'Bartleby', the book Peter gave us as a reference for his 'no-lectures'. Before engaging with the book and the famous formula, 'I would prefer not to', let us look at other possibilities to say 'no': The *Oxford English Dictionary* indicates in its blog, where it collects all the historical occurrences of the term, no less than 29 different manners.

Here they are:
1. no
2. uh-uh
3. nix
4. nixie / nixy / nixey
5. nope
6. nay
7. nah
8. no way
9. no way, José
10. negative
11. veto
12. out of the question
13. no siree
14. for foul, nor fair
15. not on your life
16. not on your Nelly
17. not on your tintype
18. not for all the tea in China
19. not in a million years
20. under no circumstances
21. not likely
22. not for Joe
23. thumbs down
24. pigs might fly
25. not a cat (in hell)'s chance
26. fat chance
27. catch me!
28. no fear
29. go fish

But what is striking with Bartleby is that he uses only one specific way to say it:

'I would prefer not to', which seemingly engages only him but, as the story shows, entails his whole environment.
What could that mean for architecture? Are we ready to take this step? Or are things to be clarified?

Laurent

Dear François,

I do not know whether this helps to clarify our topic, our approach, our hypothesis, but as we are still searching, I would like to propose another perspective on Melville's book, which I found in a text by literary scholar Leo Marx, author of a wonderful book, *The Machine in the Garden*, which you might know. The book was very useful for several researches we did, as Marx, more than others, is able to relate literature to cultural history. This is what he does also in his essay on Bartleby called 'Melville's Parable of the Walls'.

Marx does two things: first, he relates the topic to Melville's biography, pointing out that the author was, while writing 'Bartleby', in a pivotal moment in his life – a moment where his writings would shift from his very popular books to his intellectually more demanding prose, letting him fall into a crisis and obliging him to reassess his position towards himself and society.

Second, and this is perhaps more relevant for architects, he points, as the title of his essay says – why did we not see this earlier? – to the importance of walls in Melville's text. First of course, the setting in Manhattan, Wall Street, the place of the lawyer's office, where Bartleby works; but it is also a walled street, with walled rooms. Bartleby works in a room with three windows looking on three different walls: one black, one white and one without colour. This last window had previously a view. It is in front of this wall that Bartleby would stand and stare. This wall, which blocks a former 'view', separates Bartleby from society, from the Wall Street Society. It is this wall which Bartleby will look at when stopping the writing job he was assigned to do. It is again in front of a wall that Bartleby will die in prison, still staring, as he dies with open eyes.

Marx gives the following explanation for the importance of the wall as a parable in the book:

'Then why has Bartleby allowed the wall to paralyse him? The others in the office are not disturbed by the walls; in spite of the poor light they are able to do their work. Is it possible that Bartleby's suffering is, to some event, self-inflicted? that it is symptomatic of the perhaps morbid fear of annihilation manifested in his preoccupation with the dead-wall? Melville gives us reason to suspect as much [...].'

And Marx ends his essay with a comparison between the author, Melville, and Bartleby, which shows, once again, this slight difference between what you called 'projectile' and its radical, but also deadly, interpretation by Bartleby:

'Among the countless imaginative statements of the artist's problems in modern literature, 'Bartleby' is exceptional in its sympathy and hope for the average man, and in the severity of its treatment of the artist. This is particularly remarkable when we consider the seriousness of the rebuffs Melville had so recently been given by his contemporaries. But nothing, he is saying, may be allowed to relieve the writer of his obligations to mankind. If he forgets humanity, as Bartleby did, his art will die, and so will he. The lawyer, realising this, at the last moment couples Bartleby's name with that of humanity itself. The fate of the artist is inseparable from that of all men. The eerie story of Bartleby is a compassionate rebuke to the self-absorption of the artist, and so a plea that he devote himself to keeping strong his bonds with the rest of mankind. Today, exactly a century after it was written, 'Bartleby, the Scrivener' is a counter-statement to the large and ever growing canon of 'ordealist' interpretations of the situation of the modern writer.'
I hope this helps us take a step farther.

All my best,
Laurent

Dear François,

This is just a short notice.

I discovered this week three more different aspects of 'no'. It seems that our investigation will cause us some problems, as the more we think about it, the more the field opens up. But this is the general

condition of every research work.
Here, very briefly, are the three aspects: The first concerns a balance of interests, between work and family. So it is about a choice. One has to refuse one thing to be able to do another.

The second interpretation was proposed by Sarah Oppenheimer, the American artist who instantly responded to my question – how should I interpret 'no'? – that for her, 'no' meant 'slowness': the possibility to advance a work, an idea, a proposal independently from exterior pressure conditions; independently also from the modern logic of time, performance, calculable result.

The third interpretation popped up while I was preparing a lecture about the 'accident' in architecture. In this lecture, I tried to understand why the internationally acclaimed architecture of post-war Britain failed in almost every case to respond to the exigencies that were put in it: why the well-tempered space of the history faculty building in Cambridge, designed by Stirling with a heating and ventilation engineer, failed; why almost all acclaimed housing projects in Britain became at one time or another a slum. These failures may be brought back to the failure of the modern production logic. The buildings were not able to answer the calculable rationality of post-war planning. They didn't respond to the performances assigned to them. Strangely, the refusal in this case does not come from a person but from a thing. Is that possible? Looking forwards to your thoughts on this.

All my best,
Laurent

Dear Laurent,

I have the feeling – not the conviction – that *failure*, as you describe it, slightly pulls us out of our range of analysis; after all, no one really works at failing, and an object, a design or even an intention always *turns* out to be a failure only if *time* and *exterior perception* qualify it as such; this externality seems to me contradictory with the state of mind of Bartleby. And yet, your statement could also be right if one ought to consider that characters and their selective perceptions apply a judgement on Bartleby, and their afflictions towards him most definitely evolve with the timeframe of the story ... But who are we to say that Bartleby's standpoint is a *failure*? It can only be one if we consider the productive canons of our time as the only way to live, with its summoned realisation of the self as the only acceptable trajectory... not that I wished to become a Bartleby, but I can only admire his marmoreal and indisputable stance: Bartleby seems to escape judgement and is *hors du droit et du devoir*: he simply IS... and Melville doesn't justify the crashing orbit of his main character and therefore isn't judgemental of the behaviour of the strange man.

This takes me to the other two convincing points you make, namely the notion of *choice* and the struggle for *time*, both of which are central not only to the development of architecture but also to the way we lead our respective lives.

The act of *choosing* always presupposes a corollary, that of a *renouncement*; in other words, choice is always the relic of defiance, and the variables are always at least two... even when the second term is nothingness. And when we speak about a choice, the discourse necessarily triggers the awareness of its declined pendant: and here comes the famous *anterior conditional* that we all have experienced in our lives: *shouldas, couldas* and so on.

But no such thing in 'Bartleby', right? No regrets, no anterior conditional, just nothingness: admirable of bravery and of independence of mind, don't you think? No one, nor anything, will deflect him from his line of conduct, although everyone in the story tries; but it would be an all too 'cosmic' ambition – and frankly an unreasonable one – to develop a decent outline of the question of choice: too vast a topic, too personal, too.

So is the question of *time*, but allow me to try to delineate issues at stake when engaging in such a consideration. I propose that we leave aside the imprint of *time* onto architecture itself – which is indeed a fascinating topic but most likely well addressed in scientific literature – and very briefly focus on the embryonic phases of the architectural project, where *time*, or rather our relation to *time*, isn't a passive one but defines the terms of the equation of *what is yet to come*.

As opposed to the couple *time-product*, in which hardly any interdependent dynamics take place, time and *process* are on the other hand, and as we all know, resolutely entangled, the one defining to a great extent the attributes of the other. And in an era where the sole horizon seems to be short-term profit – no matter what is at stake, transgenerational or not – it becomes sadly obvious that *time* has turned into a great luxury, not in the sense of an expandable parameter, but really as an extremely rare commodity.

I have the greatest respect for those who have the strength to dictate their rhythm, and Gilles Deleuze – again – expresses it in his *ABCédaire: on ne bouscule pas un artiste!*... I don't consider architects to be artists, but issues are nevertheless similar; and I would add: *on ne bouscule pas une idée!*

Yes, as Sarah Oppenheimer suggests, the struggle for time is undoubtedly a core issue of projecting... Did you know that the SIA 102 foresees what is labelled as *recherche de parti* as the first step in the development of a project and grants it... 3% of the overall procedure! And if one considers the following phase – that of the schematic design – the percentage raises to a ridiculously modest 9%! It is like asking Tiger Wood to drive with a putting wedge!

In other words, today's consideration for one of the most crucial and perilous times in the development of an architectural project has shrunk it to hardly anything more than a glimpse of intuition opportunistically petrified in a categorical product. Some call it *pragmatism* – or worse, *realism* – when it really is *opportunism* with a short view; doubt as the necessary accessory of imagination has been brutally ruled out!
We are left with the hard edges of technocratic frameworks and today's fetishism for consumption: any nuanced resolution mobilising collective memory and criticality hardly stands any chance any more: compressed time and short-term profit have turned the project into an authoritative and unequivocal procedure.

Amitiés,
François

Dear François,

Thank you very much for your clarifications. Yesterday, another attack happened here in Paris. An outlaw driven by a destructive ideology attacked a representative of the state, of the conventional, policed order. This makes your first statement about the choice even clearer. Indeed, Bartleby is not ideological; he is not driven by others, he is not even an outlaw. He is just himself. As you say, he has no anterior condition. If he is radical, it is not in the sense that he pursues the roots, the radix of this or that, but only insofar as he goes back to the roots of the human condition. As Deleuze says in the text you recommended to me, 'Bartleby; or, the Formula', the expression 'I would prefer not to' are not so much an indication of 'things and actions', but are 'acts', 'speech-acts' in themselves. Speech-acts, as Deleuze says, are 'self- referential'. Therefore, we have also the difficulty to transpose 'I prefer not to' to architecture, literature, etc., as first and foremost, 'I prefer not to' is linked – and here again I agree with you – with a person and not a work. Deleuze again says that 'it makes Bartleby a pure outsider ('exclu') to whom no social position can be attributed'. Bartleby, through his speech-act, becomes a man 'without references'.

This quest reminded me of a difficult contradiction I wanted to resolve while writing on Valerio Olgiati's 'iconographical autobiography'. There he positions himself in relation to two pictures: Robert Ryman's white-striped *Untitled* (1965) and Helmut Federle's gold *Monochrom Untitled* (1990). Olgiati writes about the first: 'it represents nothing'; and about the second: 'it represents everything'. Obviously, one could exchange the captions, as the images are – through their radical interrogation of the state of painting (the 'it represents nothing') – a contribution to the state of painting itself (the 'it represents everything').

By this, another time dimension comes into play: not only the time of creation, the *on ne bouscule pas les artistes*. One should indeed add to this sentence: *On ne bouscule pas les oeuvres d'art*. As with 'Bartleby', every artwork tends to the infinite, which we could call the classical. Time makes this judgement: indeed, the new can become old, or it can become classical.

So much for today.

All my best,
Laurent

Dear Laurent,

I know this might seem a step backward, but if I may, I would like to share with you the passages of Deleuze's essay which interest me the most, as they are closely linked to the way we would like to think of the architectural project at Made in.

'The Confidence-Man (much as one says the Medicine-Man) is sprinkled with Melville's reflections on the novel. The first of these reflections consists in claiming the rights of a superior irrationalism. Why should the novelist believe he is obligated to explain the behaviour of his characters, and to supply them with reasons, whereas life for its part never explains anything and leaves in its creatures so many indeterminate, obscure, indiscernible zones that defy any attempt at clarification? It is life that justifies; it has no need of being justified. The English novel, and even more so the French novel, feels the need to rationalise, even if only in the final pages, and psychology is no doubt the last form of rationalism: the Western reader awaits the final word. In this regard, psychoanalysis has revived the claims of reason. (...) The founding act of the American novel, like that of the Russian novel, was to take the novel far from the order of reasons, and to give birth to characters who exist in nothingness, survive only in the void, defy logic and psychology and keep their mystery until the end. (...) What counts for a great novelist – Melville, Dostoyevsky, Kafka, or Musil – is that things remain enigmatic yet nonarbitrary: in short a new logic, definitely a logic, but one that grasps the innermost depth of life and death without leading us back to reason. The novelist has the eye of a prophet, not the gaze of a psychologist.'

Amitiés,
François

Dear François,

There is one issue we tried to escape till now. We haven't addressed history, although we have argued through our exchange with historical examples. 'Bartleby' is indeed a fiction that is placed in history. Leo Marx situates the work in Melville's life, stressing the economic context of the work published in 1853. In the text you quoted in the previous email, Deleuze also historicises the personage, even if indirectly, in comparing him to other modern figures: Modern Ulysses as he calls them, 'without a name, regicide, and parricide'. He refers the enigmatic dimension of the essay to Kafka, to Musil, to Dostoievsky.

But what would it mean to conceive of a contemporary Bartleby, and what would the 'I would prefer not to' be today? Of course, the context has changed. Probably, the resistance would be against the logics of rationalism, liberalism and administration. But how would that work? And can we still believe in the fiction of the 'work of art' and the 'artist' we have discovered throughout our exchange?

Somehow, till now, we have only been asking, 'What is 'I would prefer not to'', but shouldn't we also ask, 'Which 'I would prefer not to' is appropriate'? Or could it even be that the question is not a question anymore?

Here are a few possible ways to find an issue:
- A fiction, even a historical one, is always a tale about life. Therefore, Bartleby is contemporary.
- Bartleby's context is clearly regulated. Not by chance, the wall has a central role in Melville's story. Obviously today, we have other limits, less visible ones. In Melville, one can be outside or inside. There is no in-between. How could one deal with this threshold situation? Could the contemporary Bartleby be the flaneur, the drifter, or is it the dropout or even the hacker?
- Finally, where should one situate the work of art? Can it still be so monumental, isolated, or is it not rather an action, an intervention, that transforms its environment?

All my best, Laurent

Dear Laurent,

Quite a few questions you raise in your last message... but let us try to address some of the issues you mention; regarding the contextual framework, otherwise named *History* with a capital *H*, I personally believe that History is not simply a sententious succession of events, either condemned to obsolescence or considered with a moaning and blind allegiance (the *it was better before* syndrome); an inflexion point in history can most definitely – if not in whole at least partially – remain one after it has taken place: so, one way to embrace it would be to consider it as dynamic and therefore still potentially active or if not uplifting, then at least informative...

Specifically in the field of architecture, where the notion of progress really is devoid of any meaningful substance for the very reason that humanity's most basic and central needs have hardly evolved over time: who would seriously dare to say that, between the domus in Pompeii and the Villa Stein in Garches, a progress has taken place on an architectural level; if any at all, then on a technological level, but even that is, I think, questionable?

I sometimes have a scenery in mind when addressing issues in architecture: I move forwards looking backwards – in other words: *J'avance à reculons!* One would today rather hear: *don't look backwards, you're not going that way!* But I'd really prefer: *look backwards, you're not going that way!* Which literally makes no sense but embraces a *contradictory* dynamic, yet contradictory only in the terms. Ossip Mandelstam in *Le Bruit du Temps* has an extraordinary way to express a similar ambivalence:

My memory is not of love but of hostility and does not strive at reproducing the past but at keeping it at a distance.

And to do so, one needs a lot of memory, not a nostalgic one but a proactive and critical one; in that respect, factual knowledge is only useful insofar as it can be vectorised by an always renewed intention: in other words, knowledge is not an end but a beginning, and it should be everything but archiving!

You now see very clearly that to me the contextualisation of a given problem is indeed a relevant aspect of the understanding, but hardly ever turns into a scorched statement, which would conclusively narrow the range of its significance in the present. In other words, a given problem can potentially enter in resonance with another one, no matter how far apart these are or might well have been. Such a consideration allows me to say that a hypothetical Bartleby set in today's context would be even more extreme a posture and that his vortex-environment would be even more acutely experienced.

In *Les Feuillets d'Hypnos* (1946), René Char suggests that our heritage is devoid of any preconceived will – *Notre héritage n'est précédé d'aucun testament*. The past therefore does not leave any syntactic or grammatical reading of events... So, the real question would be: how do we proceed with it?

In the second part of your email, you dare to bring our conversation back to where Peter probably would have expected us to begin with, namely how to resist or under which circumstances does one resist?

Well, I don't think I can answer such a question, for the reasons for such behaviour are too radically specific and therefore bypass any systematic approach. I could well mention resisting moments or necessities, but it would become impoverishingly anecdotal.

Having said that, there is at least one point of which I am convinced: the most radical resistance for an architect lies in the project itself, not outside of it but literally within it; no matter how pressured or biased a decision might be, one is still free, that is one has the inalienable right to resolutely propose alternative thinking by means of projective measures. It is to me the only limit or open boundary the architect ought to accept: that of his own horizon.

And though it seems to be rather a presumptuous way to engage in a service feature – which is what architecture ultimately and indisputably is – yet there is nothing cavalier about it. The seminal stage of projection is an excess and a profusion and should never be negatively defined and constrained:

(...) a new logic, definitely a logic, but one that grasps the innermost depth of life and death without leading us back to reason.

But, of course, I realise that in today's opportunistic context, such a statement can only be perceived as suicidal or worse, ideological: yet, I personally think that it is on the contrary the most dignified way to express criticality...

Amitiés,
François

Dear François,

We had, I think, both thought that your previous email would have been the last one on our 'I prefer not to' exchange. But it raised so many questions, and disclosed so many possible misunderstandings, that I feel the need for a few remarks. I hope you will forgive me.

I guess we agree on many points: about the openness of historical knowledge, the potential of history, its informative dimension and even sometimes its authoritative character. We also agree, I think, on the notion of progress, which we might link, as you say, to technology, but surely not to architecture. And finally, we agree, as I understood, on the fact that past facts and events have per se no particular value, beside the one we are able to give them. This does not mean, of course, that history is arbitrary. It has to rely on facts, and the arguments have to be traceable. But history is not definitive. There are not only 'matters of fact', as Bruno Latour rightly stated, but also 'matters of concern'.

Therefore, a particular attention must be given to the way we look at history. In this short message, I just want to stress two ways:

- The first is what you seem to follow when you state that there are no differences between the villa at Garches and a house in Pompeii. Implicitly, this presupposes the possibility of architectural or even anthropological constants: we live, we work, we die, we have tools, we have shelters, etc., from the beginning.

- The second stresses not the constants of architecture, of human kind, of life, etc. – the 'what' –
but the different ways of dealing with them, the 'how'. It accepts chronology, but not understood as a succession of events or even a way of progress or an evolution. Rather, it is concerned with different regimes, and their way of answering the essential questions you put forward. The remarks that concluded my last contribution to our exchange were directed at this issue:

1. Melville gives a very particular setting to his story: different *milieux*, divided, separated, distinguished by different walls. In this context, trespassing one of these walls – for instance, that given by the professional milieu of the office space – is viewed as a violation.

2. Melville proposes a very particular figure: an individual without identity in the anonymity of the metropolis.

It seems to me that the architectural setting, the figure and its way of resisting – maybe even the whole cultural context in which the tale enfolds – are very much characterised by the regime of modernity: the separation between private and public, individual and society, law and outlaw, etc.

But what would it mean today? You very honestly stated that you could only answer through your individual work. This might be perfectly right for an individual confronted with an individual task to resolve. But to be free is also to understand the conditions in which one works. It seems to me, therefore, that the question should be brought to another level. What does this individual work stand for? What does it represent, or even what is represented by it? This would be the 'how'.

This is all for now; see you tomorrow.

Best,

Laurent

Intervista

An important inclination in the artistic oeuvre of Anri Sala deals with the notion of 'meaning conveyed through language', i.e. escaping the constraining and framing nature of the narrative. His first-ever piece Intervista, Finding the Words *(1998) excels at this aspiration. By confronting his mother with her anti-revisionist Marxism-Leninism political past – having endured the Albanian Communist Envar Hoxha as a young woman – an uncomfortable perspective on 'wanting to remember' and 'wanting to forget' is questioned.*

PS

Anri Sala

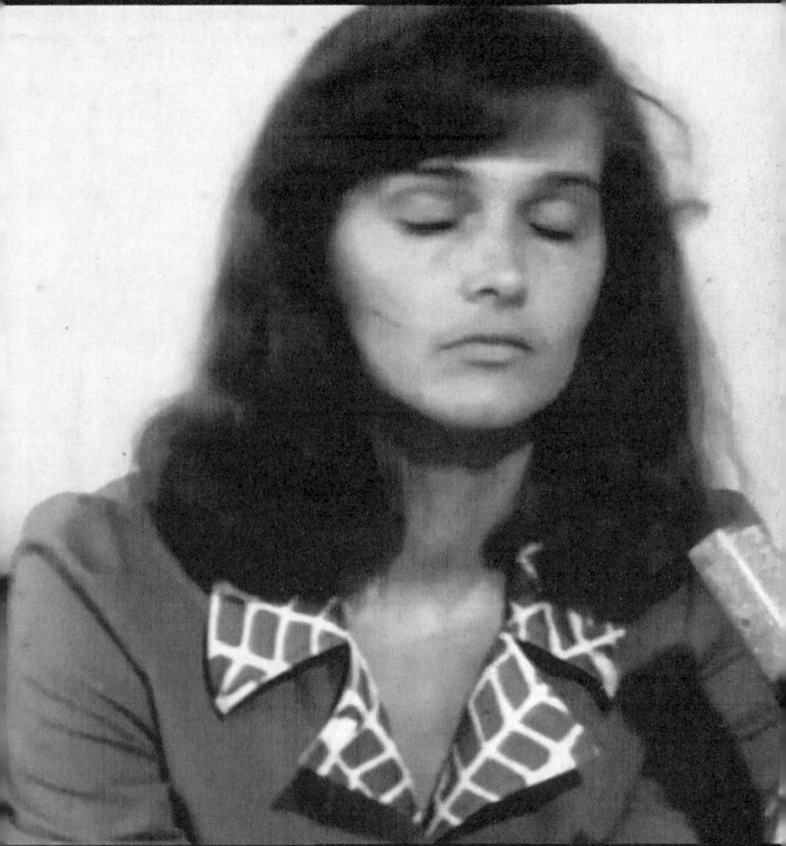

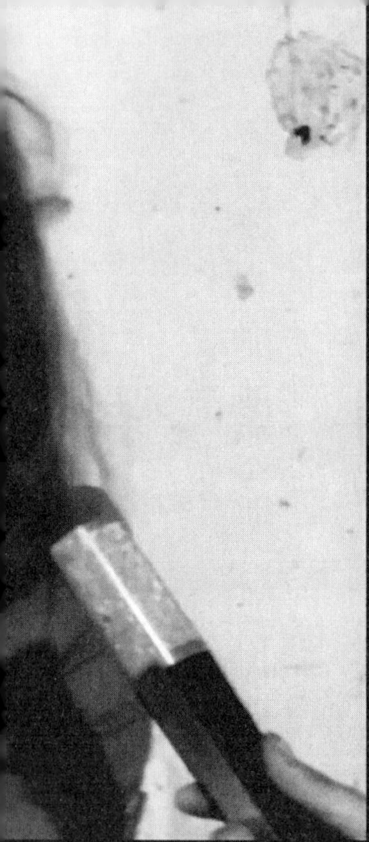

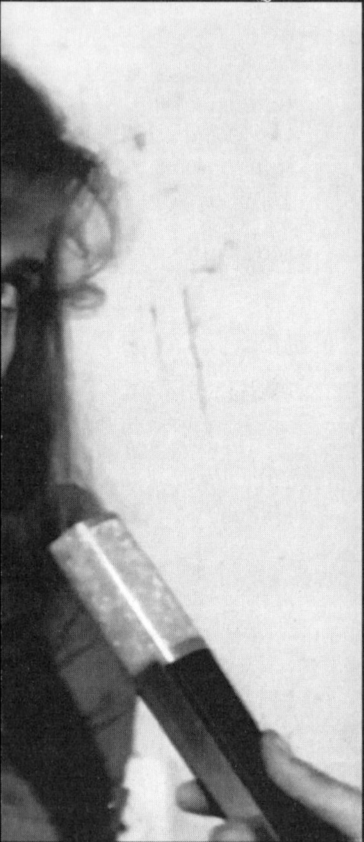

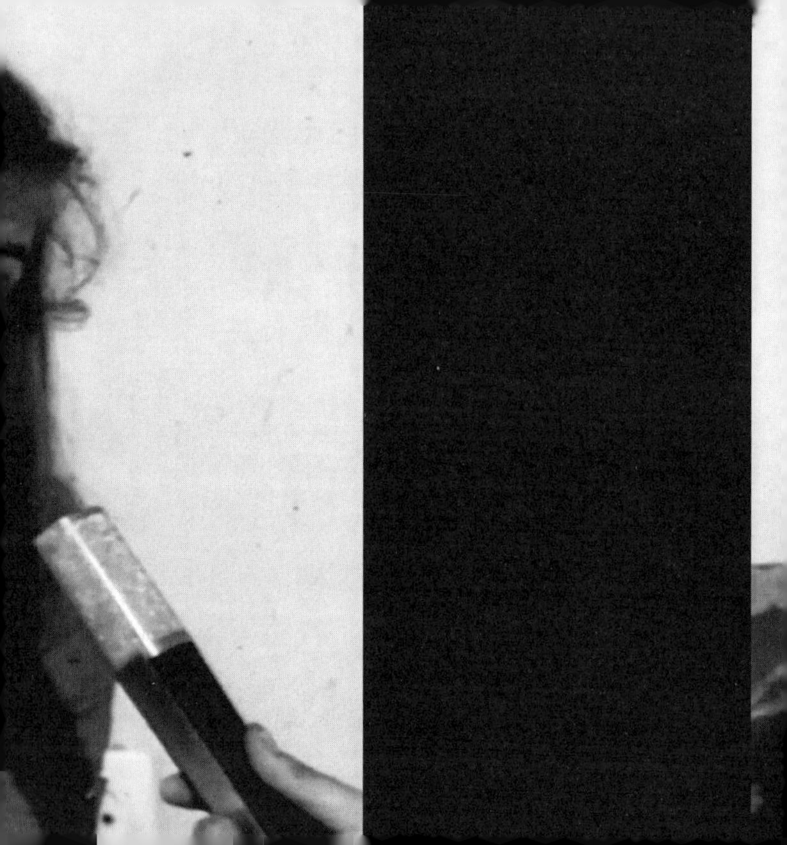

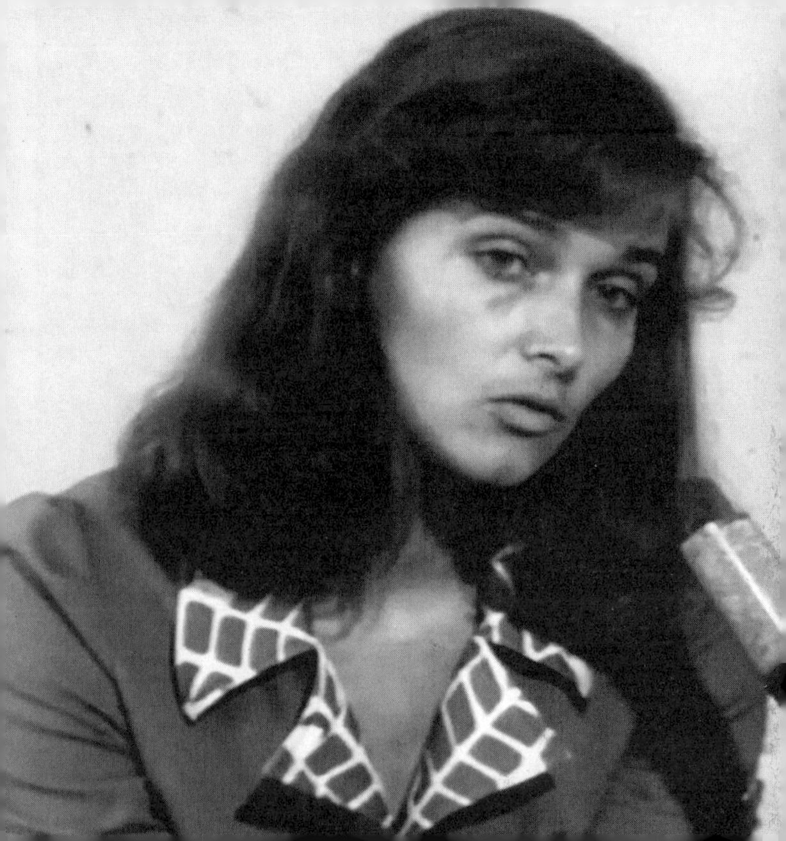

I.

How to write the history of *I Prefer Not To*? Is it conceivable to think and write a history of architecture or architects that 'preferred not to'? How to give the account of an absence of action or of the actions that stem from the wish to decline an invitation?

To explore how one could or could not write the history of 'architects that preferred not to', I return to Bartleby. In Melville's story, Bartleby the clerk or *scrivener* works for a
Master of the
ficient until th
him to assist i
a tedious job
fice. Bartleby
to; the narrato
After this first
still willing to
nothing at all.

Bartleby's
sive encroach
ning of his ap
tional positio
office consists
clerks are in o
ter opens or cl
er gets his ow
room, where i
green folding
from my sight,
thus, in a man
by works dilig
more present
master. Bartle
task at all how

Behind a High Green Folding Screen

Maarten Delbeke, Professor of the History and Theory of Architecture (ETH), trained as an architect though never took on a 'physical' position (building, designing, ...). He teaches and researches. It was this very tension he brought to the lecture hall, while re-reading Melville's novella. How to write the history of an apparent withdrawal of action, a suspicion of disengagement? And how could all this produce – in the end – a subtle gain of control?

PS

Maarten Delbeke

I.

How to write the history of *I Prefer Not To*? Is it conceivable to think and write a history of architecture or architects that 'preferred not to'? How to give the account of an absence of action or of the actions that stem from the wish to decline an invitation?

To explore how one could or could not write the history of 'architects that preferred not to', I return to Bartleby. In Melville's story, Bartleby the clerk or *scrivener* works for a Master of the Chancery. He is extremely productive and efficient until the moment when the narrator, his boss, asks him to assist in the verification of copies of legal documents, a tedious job that needs to be performed by the entire office. Bartleby declines this request by replying *I prefer not to*; the narrator is unable to convince him to act otherwise. After this first incident the number of tasks that Bartleby is still willing to perform continues to diminish, until he does nothing at all.

Bartleby's increasing passivity is matched by his progressive encroachment of his work space. From the very beginning of his appointment, Bartleby had occupied an exceptional position in the office. The Master of the Chancery's office consists of two rooms, separated by sliding doors; the clerks are in one room, the narrator in the other, and the latter opens or closes the doors as he seems fit. Bartleby however gets his own small table against the wall of the narrator's room, where it is hidden behind a screen. *I procured a high green folding screen, which might entirely isolate Bartleby from my sight, though not remove him from my voice. And thus, in a manner, privacy and society were conjoined.* Bartleby works diligently, almost without moving, so that he is no more present than a piece of furniture at the disposal of his master. Bartleby's increasing unwillingness to perform any task at all however transforms this near invisibility into an ever growing, ineluctable and destabilizing presence. Melville describes the surprise and astonishment of clients who find in the room of the narrator a clerk who does not work.

The true measure of Bartleby's presence only emerges when the narrator discovers that Bartleby actually lives in his own office. The narrator had already noted that Bartleby was always present on work days: *he was always there*. But when he decides to visit the office on a Sunday, his attempt to enter is met by Bartleby opening the door in shirtsleeves and slightly disheveled, who asks the narrator to return sometime later as he, Bartleby, still has business to attend to. Entirely flabbergasted, the narrator leaves but eventually comes back. By then Bartleby has left. Inside, the narrator discovers to his shock traces of Bartleby's domestic life in the nooks and crannies of the office.

> *Upon more closely examining the place, I surmised that for an indefinite period Bartleby must have ate, dressed and slept in my office, and that, too, without plate, mirror or bed. The cushioned seat of a rickety old sofa in one corner bore the faint impress of a lean, reclining form. Rolled away under his desk I found a blanket; under the empty grate, a blacking box and brush; on a chair, a tin basin, with soap and a ragged towel; in a newspaper a few crumbs of gingernuts and a morsel of cheese.*

This discovery reverses the relationship between the narrator and Bartleby completely. Irritation about Bartleby's gentle but stubborn refusal to work morphs into sincere concern about the situation and about Bartleby himself:

> *Yes, thought I, it is evident enough that Bartleby has been making his home here, keeping bachelor's hall all by himself. Immediately then the thought came sweeping across me, what miserable friendlessness and lone-*

liness are here revealed! His poverty is great; but his solitude, how horrible! Think of it. Of a Sunday, Wall-street is deserted as Petra; and every night of every day it is an emptiness. This building too, which of week-days hums with industry and life, at nightfall echoes with sheer vacancy, and all through Sunday is forlorn. And here Bartleby makes his home; sole spectator of a solitude which he has seen all populous–a sort of innocent and transformed Marius brooding among the ruins of Carthage! For the first time in my life a feeling of overpowering stinging melancholy seized me.

The story suggests a proportional relationship between Bartleby's inaction and his appropriation of the office, of his impassive presence and the total identification of his living and working space, where neither a life or work seem to be taking place. The process ends in an insoluble deadlock. That Bartleby's entire life unfolds in the office space leads to *overpowering melancholy* in the narrator, but also to rebellion of the other clerks, and the compulsive use of the verb *to prefer* (characterized as a *strange 'word'*) by all involved. Ultimately the narrator attempts to end the predicament by moving his office to another location, where the old regime of work and hierarchy can be reestablished. But there he is chased by the new tenants of his former rooms, as Bartleby remains firmly in place. In an ultimate attempt to deflect destiny, the narrator offers the clerk to live in his own house, thereby completing, implicitly, the identification of domestic space and work space that Bartleby's impassivity instated. Bartleby refuses, and as the narrator feared, he is arrested by the police and thrown into jail. Despite the narrator's best efforts, Bartleby dies there a few days later.

The process by which Bartleby's life progressively coincides with his refusal to act and the appropriation of the office pertains to our question: how to write the history of 'I prefer not to'? Bartleby's situation establishes a tense relationship between what can be ascertained, verified and narrated – what is present and can be transformed into history – and what remains hidden and unsaid. On the one hand there is Bartleby sitting at this desk doing nothing: performing no action, generating no story; and there is a hidden life unfolding in the same space, invisible, without attributes and objects: it can only be imagined, and then only incompletely. The concealed and lonely life of Bartleby in the rooms left empty after work complements the suspended utterance 'I prefer not to.' The suppressed verb or conjunction mirrors the hidden life that takes place outside the view of the narrator or the reader of the story, while both the hidden life and the inaction weigh ineluctably on the office room.

The problem posed by Bartleby, the fact that his life is not part of a history, is exactly what the narrator declares at the beginning of the short story:

> *While of other law-copyists I might write the complete life, of Bartleby nothing of that sort can be done. I believe that no materials exist for a full and satisfactory biography of this man. It is an irreparable loss to literature. Bartleby was one of those beings of whom nothing is ascertainable, except from the original sources, and in his case those are very small. What my own astonished eyes saw of Bartleby, that is all I know of him, except, indeed, one vague report which will appear in the sequel.*

The point made here is encapsulated in the sentence: 'What my own astonished eyes saw of Bartleby, that is all I know of him.' The most lasting imprint that Bartleby appears to have made beyond what could be immediately observed is in *the cushioned seat of a rickety old sofa in one corner, which bore the faint impress of a lean, reclining form.* Even his writings consisted only of copies of other texts, and also these traces disappear with his increasing refusal to work. As a consequence, it is impossible to write his history or biography. There are no elements, indications, sources, actions that link the singularity of Bartleby's life to anything other than his existence in the room of the office. Bartleby's life unfolds not at the intersection of other lives, events, story lines, ... but within the closed confines of an unproductive residency. Outside, there is literally no life; when Bartleby is removed, he dies.

II.

Architectural history is inevitably bound up with biography, with the life and actions of architects. Refusal, polite but firm, can well occur in a biography, but a biography can't be made of refusal alone. In fact, when refusal occurs in a biography, it generally serves to strengthen the narrative of action, virtue and success, as the following example illustrates.

It concerns Gian Lorenzo Bernini (1598-1680), the sculptor, architect and painter active in Rome from his teenage years until his death, and responsible for much of what we associate today with the Roman baroque. After a meteoric career which brought Bernini to the fulcrum of the papal court, the pontificate of Innocent X Pamphili (r. 1644–55) and the failure of the project of building the bell towers of St. Peter's led to a period of disgrace. According to the two biographies published shortly after Bernini's death, this misfortune inspired the artist to create a sculptural group representing Truth unveiled by Time, an artistic statement that his reputation would eventually be vindicated. According to a letter written in 1647, the finished group would have looked as follows:

> *The idea is of [Time] who, flying, tears down buildings and similar things and unveils the truth. There you will see a human figure, larger than life-size, who with most beautiful art will seem to fly. There you will see*

Bernini, *Truth Unveiled by Time*,1652

the difference between the symmetry of a man and of a woman, the difference of the face and the complexion of an old man and a young woman. There will be space to show something of architecture and bas relief as well.

Bernini sculpted the figure of Truth, which is now in the Villa Borghese. But, as Bernini's youngest son and biographer Domenico writes, the figure of Time 'in the act of revealing Truth' was never made.

Although the Cavaliere [Bernini] had seen to the procurement of a large and most beautiful block of marble in order to create the figure of Time–but either it was the disdain of Time itself (which ever in motion by its own nature did not wish to be eternalized through the hands of Bernini) or some other serious preoccupation, that kept the work [on the stone] at a distance–that which was marble remained stone, quarried in vain and useless.

Bernini's other biographer, Filippo Baldinucci, is more succinct when he explains why Bernini never made the statue of Time, attributing it to 'his other occupations'. Yet in his biography he included a poem he wrote about the untouched block of marble, which has the stone bemoan its fate and recall how it was taken by Bernini from an 'ancient cliff' to be given 'voice and spirit' and 'movement and flight'. Yet right when the sculptor's hand was ready to administer the 'life-giving strokes' and realize the 'thought' his 'mind' had conceived, Bernini mused to himself whether it makes sense to 'reveal ... Glories offering themselves to a cruel tyrant [Time]' when he, Bernini, is 'accustomed' to 'rendering heroes eternal' with his art? Should Time be placated by offering him monuments on which to feast? Bernini concluded not, as virtue will remain 'intact' regardless of the passing of time. His attention turned away, and the block remained 'mere stone.'

Domenico and Baldinucci both acknowledge that Bernini's project never came to fruition and attribute this failure to Time's resistance to sculpture. According to Domenico, the very fleetingness of Time rendered the operation impossible; for Baldinucci, Time is the greatest enemy of the eternity to which virtue aspires. In both cases, Time's issues with eternity are exemplified by its problematic relationship with stone, either because Time does not allow itself to be captured by it, or because Time tends to devour the stone 'glories' that honor and commemorate virtue.

We know that the unworked stone quarried for Time remained conspicuously visible in front of his house during Bernini's lifetime. Baldinucci's poem thus gave voice to an object that was as present in Bernini's surroundings as the finished statue of Truth, which remained in the artist's studio until his death. If the presence of the unworked stone might come across as a permanent reminder of failure, in the end it worked as a claim for Bernini's authority over Time. By withholding from Time the transformative powers he lavished on the figure of Truth, Bernini cast himself, rather than Time, as the great revealer. The unworked stone is a monument to refusal and, as such, a radical celebration of creative power. Bernini, not Time, choses what to reveal and how to write history.

The example of Bernini shows how a possibly hesitant refusal becomes an affirmative act, a positive statement. It is not just one moment amongst many others marking a successful Life, but almost its emblematic achievement, embodied in the rock in front of Bernini's house. Such achievement is however only possible when the refusal is an exception. As such, it vindicates the other moments when the main protagonist said YES.

The question of how refusal shapes or undermines the history of artists and their oeuvres is a matter of architecture, of how architects see themselves in history. Do they allow their refusals to delineate their oeuvre, as a backlight to their achievements, do the refusals disappear from view, or are they an intrinsic part of their work? But it is also an issue of historiography, of how we choose to write history, and the imperative that history has something to do with traces, actions and deeds, and realizations; and of the historian's own ambiguous relationship to action, especially in the field of architecture, as someone who prefers not to design or to build, but to research, write and teach.

The narrator of Bartleby is a perfect stand-in for the historian – an observer perplexed by the absence of motivation, of actions, of traces, of a life; moved to deep melancholy for so much nothing, as it eludes his grasp and can only point at lonely desolation. But what if Bartleby were the historian, much like Bernini? Melville's story actually contains some ground for this assertion. At the very end of the story the narrator imparts the single snippet of information he managed to collect about Bartleby's previous life, nothing more than a rumor:

> *Yet here I hardly know whether I should divulge one little item of rumor, which came to my ear a few months after the scrivener's decease. Upon what basis it rested, I could never ascertain; and hence, how true it is I cannot now tell. But inasmuch as this vague report has not been without certain strange suggestive interest to me, however sad, it may prove the same with some others; and so I will briefly mention it. The report was this: that Bartleby had been a subordinate clerk in the Dead Letter Office at Washington, from which he had been suddenly removed by a change in the administration. When I think over this rumor, I cannot adequately express the emotions which seize me. Dead letters! does it not sound like dead men? Conceive a man by nature and misfortune prone to a*

pallid hopelessness, can any business seem more fitted to heighten it than that of continually handling these dead letters, and assorting them for the flames? For by the cart-load they are annually burned. Sometimes from out the folded paper the pale clerk takes a ring– the finger it was meant for, perhaps, moulders in the grave; a bank-note sent in swiftest charity:–he whom it would relieve, nor eats nor hungers any more; pardon for those who died despairing; hope for those who died unhoping; good tidings for those who died stifled by unrelieved calamities. On errands of life, these letters speed to death. Ah Bartleby! Ah humanity!

Collecting and dispensing bits of histories; histories that are perhaps written but never received or recorded, dead ends that disappear. This experience is what Bartleby brings to the office, as the one who politely refuses to take part in the daily life around him, and sits, increasingly immobile, at a small table right next to the action.

Bartleby as an architectural historian epitomizes the idea that doing history originates in and consists of an act of refusal. If architecture is the ultimate YES profession, architectural history might be the I PREFER NOT TO option. Especially in the case of historians of architecture who trained as architects but prefer not to build, and to cast away years of education in structural engineering and soil mechanics to venture into a field for which they are barely trained at all. Who forfeit the pleasure of making things in the real world. Bartleby invites us to think of architectural history as a practice defined by refusal.

What would such a refusal mean? Bartleby's progressive withdrawal from work is proportional to the increasing identification with his room; his passivity increases his presence, not as an active agent but as something that perhaps resembles Bernini's unmade statue of Time: a rock that sits there. It is as an obstacle that Bartleby elicits increasingly frenetic activity, a torrent in the words of the narrator, from the upheaval in the office, over the move of the narrator to other premises and all subsequent vicissitudes, to the final events of Bartleby's eventual removal, imprisonment and death. With this torrent comes the increasingly tormented examination of conscience of the narrator, who incessantly ponders the morality and effectiveness of his own actions.

Perhaps the key point is that from the outset the narrator chose to share his room with Bartleby. He invited the clerk to share a space occupied by a man of action, behind a *high green folding screen, which might entirely isolate Bartleby from my sight, though not remove him from my voice.* Strikingly, Melville adds that thus, in a manner, *privacy and society were conjoined.* It is in this constellation, between the sociable and the utterly solitary, that Bartleby the historian does his work. Not as a scrivener, but as someone whose passive presence challenges what can be ascertained, written down or said.

References

All quotes are taken from Melville's *Bartleby, the Scrivener,* unless indicated otherwise.

The two biographies of Bernini are:
Filippo Baldinucci, *Vita del cavaliere Gio: Lorenzo Bernino scultore, architetto, e pittore, scritta da Filippo Baldinucci fiorentino*, Florence, 1682.

Domenico Bernini, *Vita del Cavalier Gio. Lorenzo Bernino, descritta da Domenico Bernino suo figlio,* Rome, 1713.

The letter with the description of Bernini's intended *Truth unveiled by Time* was published by Madeleine Laurain-Portemer, "Mazarin et le Bernin. À propos du Temps, qui decouvre la Vérité," *Gazette des Beaux-Arts* 74 (1969): 185-200.

My discussion of Bernini's refusal to sculpt Time has been published previously in "The matter of metaphor. Truth, sculpture and the word," in Evonne Levy, Carolina Mangone (eds), *Material Bernini* (Milton Park: Routledge, 2016), 23–38.

THE PU
CAN
AND EN

6 Public Lessons

It is quite easy to forget any form of real public engagement and ditto practice in the protected environment that is the ETH campus (or even Switzerland for that matter). For this reason, it was all the more relevant to invite someone like Finn Williams and his Public Practice.

Based on a renewed creed for public architectural practice the organization represents a non-profit social enterprise with the clear mission to improve the quality and equality of everyday places. Through six 'lessons' Finn Williams problematized their pitch, setting the scene for a wide gamut of potential public practices.

PS

Finn Williams

THE RU
BE DES

SHAPING PLACES
MEANS SHAPING
DECISION MAKING

THE RU
BE DES

PLANNING
ES CAN
IGNED
ES
Y

GOO
EVERYDA
CA
EXTRA

D PLANNING
Y PLACES
N BE
RDINARY

O PLANNING
ATES NEW
ORTUNITIES

PLANNING
DEMOC

BUILDS
ACY

Entering the Field of Policy-Making is a Work of Design

What if the (confabulated) design innocence is shed, and the architect gets into politics? For better or for worse. Brandlhuber performing as Brandlhuber. A final stage before entering politics himself?

PS

חזק בביטחון.
חזק בכלכלה.
הליכוד
News
Benjamin Netanyahu
(1949-)
Image: Financial Times

Springfield Republican
25 Cents
WAR ENDS—TOTAL ISRAEL VICTORY
Syrians Collapse In Final Campaign; UN Session Called
U. S. Pilots Hit Power Complex
Resignation of Vance Stirs Up Washington
Ladybird Guest At Clambake
1967 – 1972
Member of Sayeret Matkal,
a Israeli special force.
Source: http://radical-pedagogies.com
Image: http://israelalbum.org

1972 – 1976
B.Sc. in Architecture & M.Sc in
Business Managment
MIT Boston
Source: The Prime Minister's Office (Israel)
Image: Nick Allen CC-BY-SA 4.0

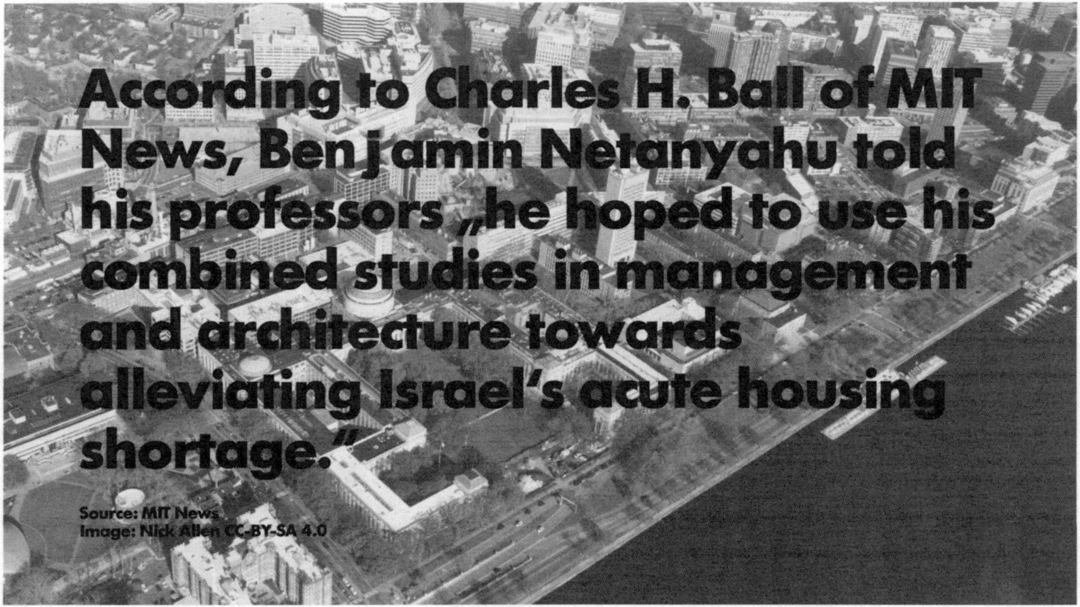
According to Charles H. Ball of MIT News, Benjamin Netanyahu told his professors „he hoped to use his combined studies in management and architecture towards alleviating Israel's acute housing shortage."
Source: MIT News
Image: Nick Allen CC-BY-SA 4.0

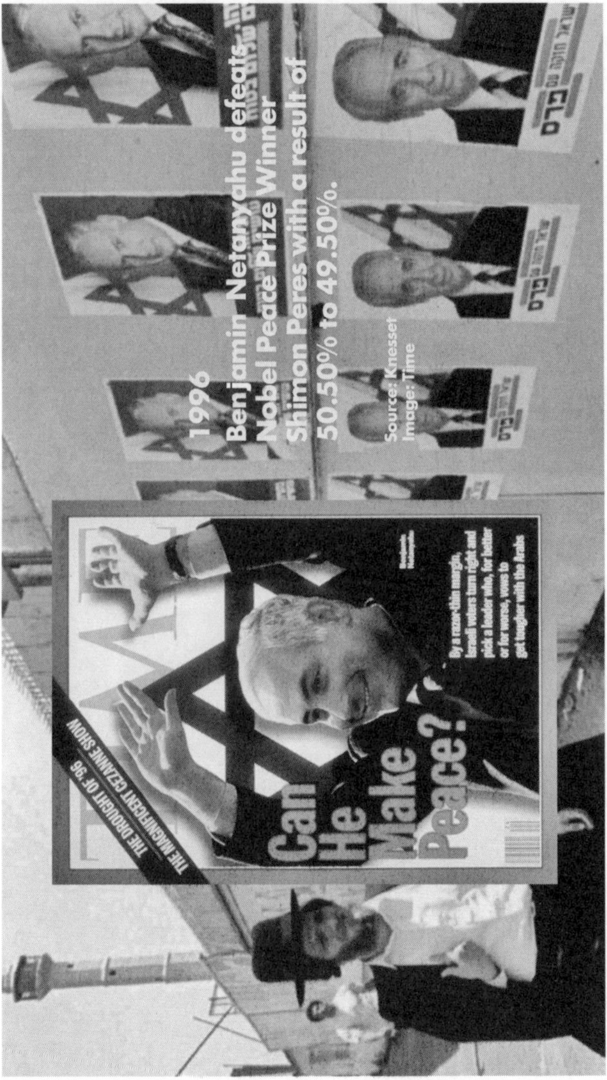
1996
Benjamin Netanyahu defeats Nobel Peace Prize Winner Shimon Peres with a result of 50.50% to 49.50%.
Source: Knesset
Image: Time
TIME
THE MAGNIFICENT CEZANNE SHOW
THE DROUGHT OF '96
Can He Make Peace?
By a razor-thin margin, Israeli voters turn right and pick a leader who, for better or for worse, vows to get tougher with the Arabs

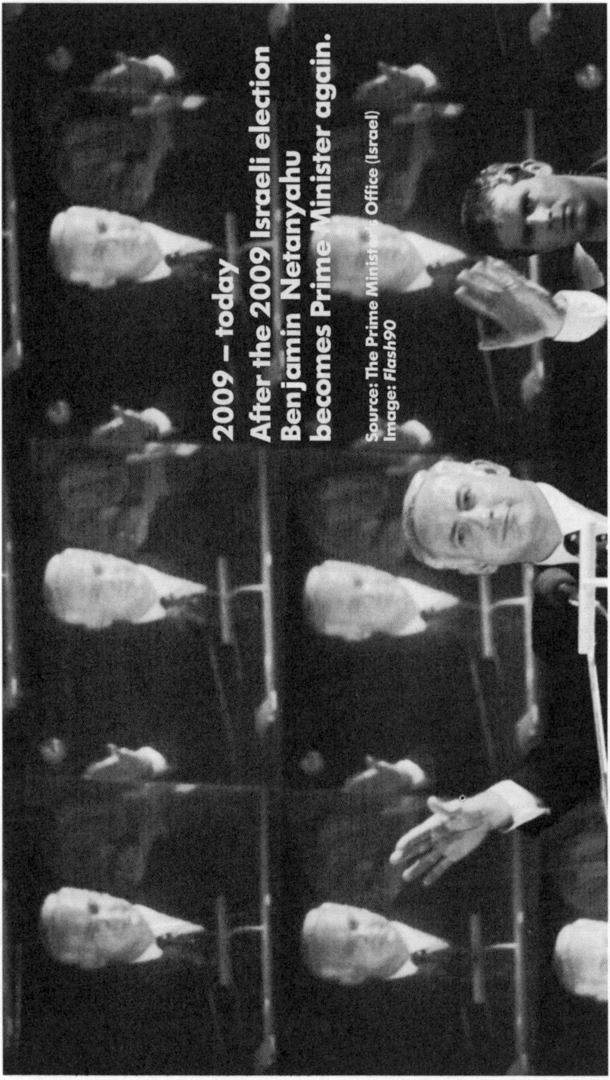

2009 – today
After the 2009 Israeli election Benjamin Netanyahu becomes Prime Minister again.

Source: The Prime Minister's Office (Israel)
Image: *Flash90*

Israeli Prime Minister Benjamin Netanyahu drawing the red line, to warn Iran about an pre-emptive strike.

Quelle: Israel Ministry of Foreign Affairs
Bild: Haaretz

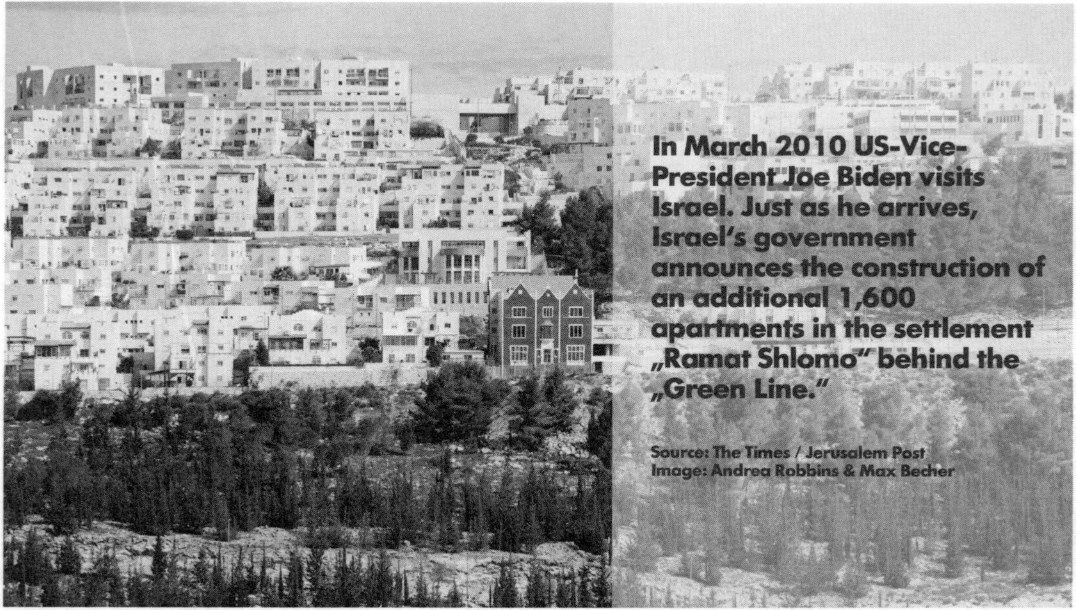
In March 2010 US-Vice-President Joe Biden visits Israel. Just as he arrives, Israel's government announces the construction of an additional 1,600 apartments in the settlement „Ramat Shlomo" behind the „Green Line."
Source: The Times / Jerusalem Post
Image: Andrea Robbins & Max Becher

Anca Petrescu
(*1949 in Schäßburg, Romania)
Image: rtv.net

1973
Diploma in Architecture at Ion Mincu University of Architecture and Urbanism (IAIM) Bucharest with a project on Bucharest's central „Arsenalhill."
Source: Dana Vais: The (In)famous Anca Petrescu
Image: rtv.net

1977

Nicolae Ceaușescu took the chance and launched the „Competition for the restructuring of Bucharest's City Center." For the construction site three historic districts on Arsenalhill were demolished.

Source: telegraph.co.uk
Image: Petre Dumitrescu / AGERPRES ARHIVA

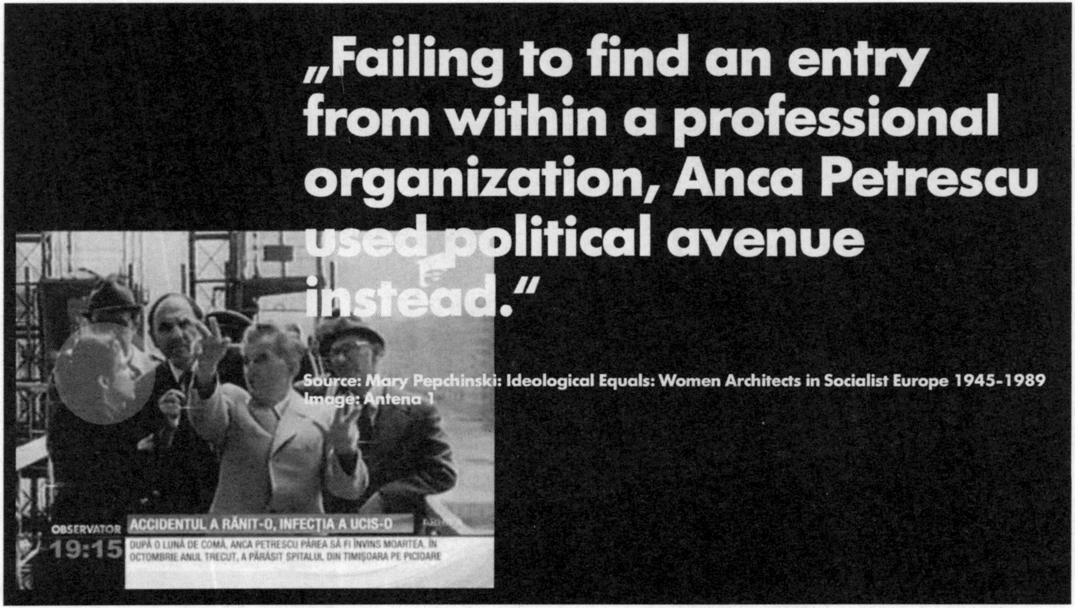
„Failing to find an entry from within a professional organization, Anca Petrescu used political avenue instead.“
Source: Mary Pepchinski: Ideological Equals: Women Architects in Socialist Europe 1945-1989
Image: Antena 1
OBSERVATOR
19:15
ACCIDENTUL A RĂNIT-O, INFECȚIA A UCIS-O
DUPĂ O LUNĂ DE COMĂ, ANCA PETRESCU PĂREA SĂ FI ÎNVINS MOARTEA. ÎN OCTOMBRIE ANUL TRECUT, A PĂRĂSIT SPITALUL DIN TIMIȘOARA PE PICIOARE

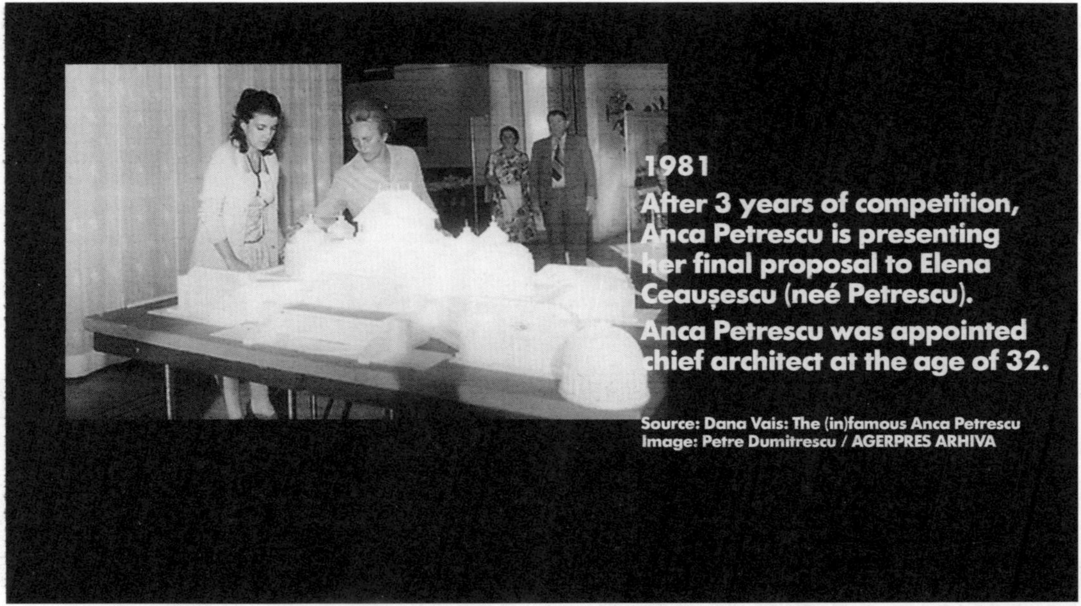
1981
After 3 years of competition, Anca Petrescu is presenting her final proposal to Elena Ceaușescu (neé Petrescu).
Anca Petrescu was appointed chief architect at the age of 32.
Source: Dana Vais: The (in)famous Anca Petrescu
Image: Petre Dumitrescu / AGERPRES ARHIVA

1984
Approximately one million Romanians, including military conscripts, political prisoners and a team of 700 architects, worked round the clock under Anca Petrescu on the construction site.
Source: telegraph.co.uk
Image: Petre Dumitrescu / AGERPRES ARHIVA

1989

Nicolae Ceaușescu's public execution also means the end of any building activity.

Source: Dana Vais: The (in)famous Anca Petrescu
Image: Televiziunea Romana

1989 – 2003
Anca Petrescu is forced to leave Romania. She is working as an architect for Club Med, Florida.
Source: Schediwy, Robert: Städtebilder: Reflexionen zum Wandel in Architektur und Urbanistik
Image: Club Med

2004
Anca Petrescu runs for office with far-right and ultranationalist PRM Party.

Source: Dana Vais: The (in)famous Anca Petrescu
Image: ---

2004 – 2008
As a member of Parliament Anca Petrescu declares that she ran for office only to receive permanent access to the building, that houses the parliament since 1994.

Source: Dana Vais: The (in)famous Anca Petrescu
Image: Razvan Chirta / Medaifox Foto

2014

Anca Petrescu died in a car accident in Bucharest. Her body was layed out in People's Palace for a ceremony before the burial.

Source: Romania TV
Image: Romania TV

Bogdan
Bogdanović
(*1922,
Beograd)
Image: Financial Times

1940-1950
Enrolled in the University of Belgrade, Faculty of Engineering, Department of Architecture.
Source: World Architecture
Image: Univerzitet u Beogradu

At the end of WWII Bogdan Bogdanović as a partisan is participating „a little bit" in the liberation of Jugoslavija.

Source: Die Zeit
Image: SFRJ

Smrt fasizmu sloboda Narodu! Death to fascism, freedom to the people! Young yugoslav partisans in 1943.

Jansenovac: Memorial on site of the former concentration camp (1971)
1952 – 1981
Bogdan Bogdanović built several memorials, mainly dedicated to the Yugoslav Partisans of WWII.
Source: World Architecture
Image: Robert Burghardt

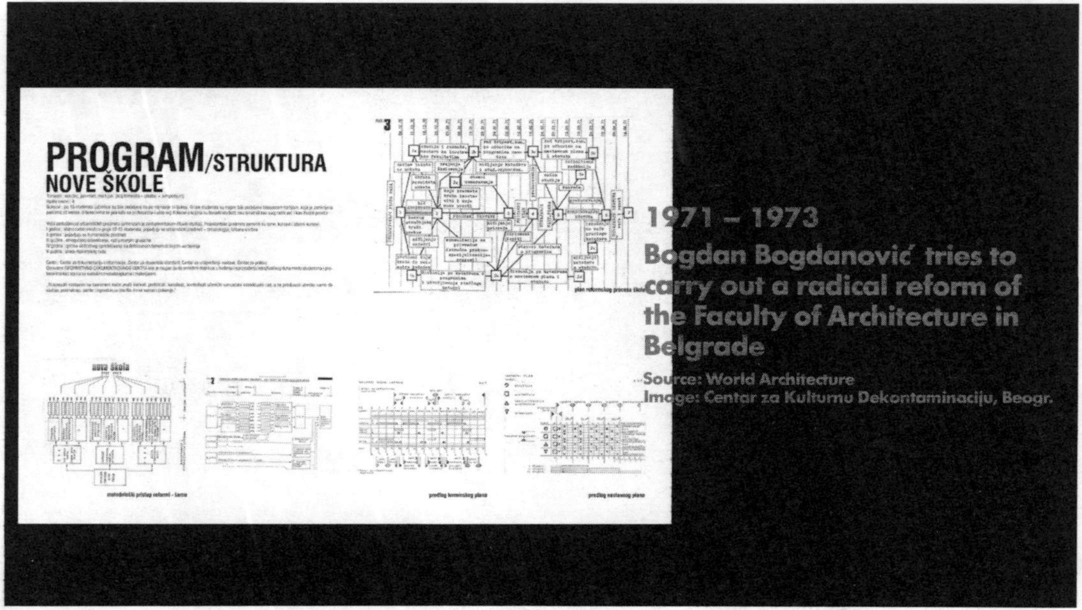
PROGRAM/STRUKTURA
NOVE ŠKOLE
plan reformskog procesa škole
nova škola
metodološki pristup reformi - šema
predlog kurikularnog plana
predlog nastavnog plana
1971 – 1973
Bogdan Bogdanović tries to carry out a radical reform of the Faculty of Architecture in Belgrade
Source: World Architecture
Image: Centar za Kulturnu Dekontaminaciju, Beogr.

1977

Bogdan Bogdanović transfers his study course „Symbolic Forms" to Mali Popović, a village near Belgrade and forms the „School of Architecture Philosophy"

Source: World Architecture
Image: Bogdan Bogdanović

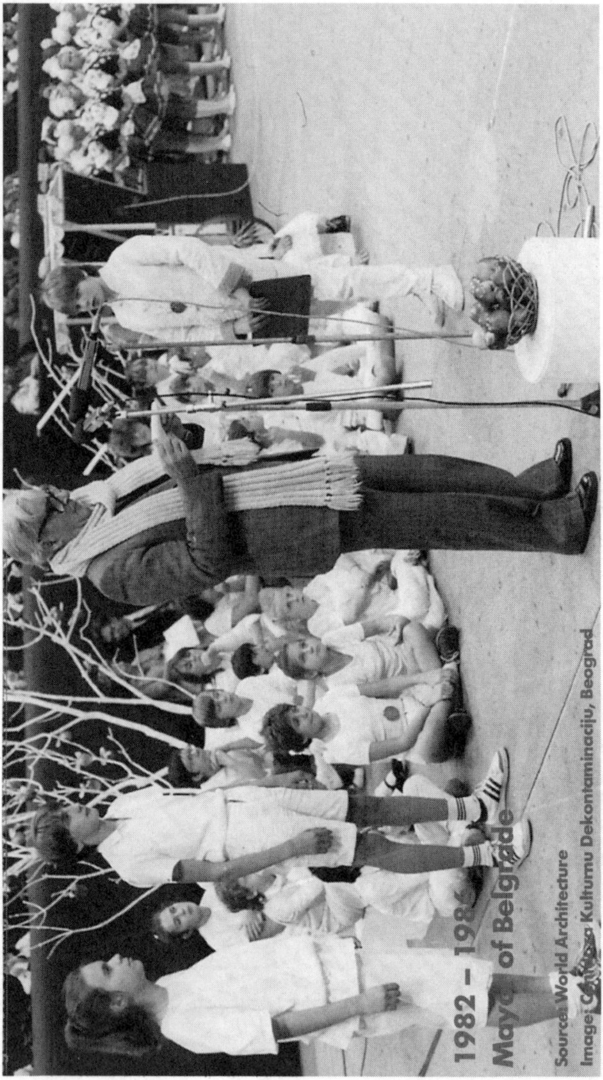
1982 – 198
of Belgrade
Source: World Architecture
Image: Kulturnu Dekontaminaciju, Beograd

1987

Slobodan Milošević gives the historic speech at Kosovo Polje that marks the radical shift from Titoism to Nationalism.

Source: Mldaost
Image: Mladost

1987

Open letter to the Serbian Communist Party and retirement of all official functions.

Source: Mldaost
Image: Mladost

1993 – 2010
Exile in Vienna.
Source: ---
Image: ---
dtv
Bogdan Bogdanović
Der verdammte Baumeister
Erinnerungen

A Conversation with Students

Wrapping up two years of ETH studio teaching, thematically built around architecture and policy whispering strategies, Studio Swinnen held a final conversation at the forested edge of the ETH Hönggerberg Campus. An open-ended discussion on risk-taking, finding freedoms, proactivity, doubt, ghostwriting, the architect as producer and even boredom as thriving energies for operating space. Students becoming the guides.

PS

ETH Studio Swinnen

Participants: Oliver Burch
Lauro Foletti
Tobias Häusermann
Tobias Hentzer
Dausgaard
Lukas Graf
Sophie Keel
Oscar Lussi
Lea Maeder
Jasmin Mahr
Philippe Nathan
Mathis Pante
Noël Picco
Ina Stammberger
Magdalena Stolze
Lukas Stadelmann
Peter Swinnen
Mélissa Vrolixs

PS
The past two years the studio focused on detecting 'cracks in the system', or how to infiltrate political decision processes through the use of architecture. How to find freedoms within and for the architectural discipline? Perhaps we should recalibrate 'the architect' as a producer instead of a self-fulfilling divine creator or designer? What's your reading of such a propositional practice?

OL
In general, debating architecture in a public and political manner is far too absent within education. I feel that at the ETH architectural department there's no real societal discussion. We should be more political.

PS
What does that entail? Taking on a more proactive stand?

OL
Maybe clearly taking the initiative is a first point for change to arise. Often, it's not clear who is supposed to take the initiative. Change is never producing itself.

LS
There's also a danger of course. The danger of the architect as a 'proactive' moral high ground, overlooking it all, knowing everything ... To a certain degree, I could agree with your first move on 'proactivity' as a potential motor for the architectural discipline, though I equally detect a significant risk. Especially combined with the very type of education we get at ETH, very distant from reality, as being in an ideal bubble. We feel distanced

from other disciplines. Literally, the campus lies on a forested hill completely outside of the city core of Zurich.

THD
I read your provocation on 'proactivity' as taking on the risk to produce an urgent concept without specifically being asked to. Architecture as an unsolicited practice. And the capacity for a necessary level of generosity towards the public interest that can come from this.

PS
Isn't the contemporary architect reduced to an ideal or idealized executor? At best you're a capable executor of a more or less interesting brief. That is the best to hope for, if proactivity doesn't come into play.

OL
With a beautifying and estheticizing reflex as the ultimate architectural tool...? I do believe that your suggestion on proactivity in architecture is an interesting one ...

PS
But an extremely naïve one!

OL
Indeed, a very naïve one. Though it holds a certain urgency and impactful promise to it. Like an anarchistic approach of sorts.

PS
I understand 'naïve' as in relationship to an eventual state of authorship. A proactive practice often needs

to happen under the radar—at first—and hence, it could be considered as a form of ghostwriting. Giving up authorship within the architectural discipline is truly naïve, but I often feel it's the only way ahead. It entails intervening at the pre-start of a project, writing the brief if you wish, and using architectural processes to help detect the actual questions and urgencies at hand. The very moment you can whisper ideas into ears of the powers that be, actors that aren't necessarily able to decode how architecture can address a societal need. This whispering is evidently not an innocent practice, using architecture as a positive manipulation tool. All in all, this type of practice is quite different from trying to control the last 'architectural detail' on a construction site. Do you see this as a potential?

THD
It can be about simple things, in my understanding. For instance trying to influence how public a ground floor level will be, something that surpasses pure aesthetic considerations or any commercial a priori. It's about inducing public benefits.

LS
Such 'self-initiative' is evidently not a new concept within the architectural practice. It happens all the time. At the same time I see how superficially architecture is perceived publically, in the press, ... the outperformed 'starchitects' for instance. Such misconception on architecture prohibits a truly relevant practice.

MS
The drive for proactivity is actually very alive amongst students, though it's not fully being pushed.

IS
We recently set up a studio ourselves, without professors. So that option is available! Though you have to put it on the table yourself, of course. A lingering problematic remains the culture of ego-driven architects that are teaching us. And the fact that the Dean changes every two years is destabilizing things too much. Hence, the department of architecture is incapable of formulating a clear position.

PS
So this quest, almost lust, for proactivity is apparently already embedded amongst students?

MS
I believe it is expected.

PS
By whom? What for?

MS
Architecture should be a critical practice. This seems to be the implicit expectation all over.

OL
Questioning things, that seems to be the point. Though that's something you have to learn.

PS
All depends on how you value architecture in the end. I consider it by default a critical 'service profession', able to problematize, instead of pretending to solve.

MS
Is it?

PS
It implies a service to society.

THD
Architecture is about the power of proposing something, often in an unsolicited manner. That is the positivism of architecture. The lecture series I Prefer Not To, that you recently staged at ETH, reinforces this in my view. In the resisting or postponing of a designer-like judgment lies equally the crucial proposal and its societal strength.

PS
I Prefer Not To aimed at surpassing any yes/no binary. Of 'simply' being in or out. Not all of the installments reached such clarity of course. Talking about binaries, last night I watched a streamed Berlin lecture by OMA/Rem Koolhaas. Before elaborating the firm's recent projects, mainly in China and Qatar, he uttered the following antagonism: 'We prefer sympathy over (Western) moralism.' A statement serving to dispute any potential critique on their work for autocratic regimes. Unfortunately, it was but a lecture, so without any real debate on the subject afterwards. Why should architectural practice be so reductive? And sympathy is of course not an innocent position.

MS
I think Koolhaas might be right here. Those projects are a test of our sympathy.

PS
Those projects are mainly tests for pushing clients, at best creating some sort of public value through hyper-investments.

THD
The issue of the client, and how to positively manipulate this actor needs to be broached through a very positive attitude. Perhaps it's more about discovering a variety of clients we haven't thought about so far. In order to guarantee a maximum effect for public interest.

LS
The client as a tool is an intriguing thought.

THD
On the other side of the spectrum, a lot of bottom-up practices are currently hailed as the ideal way to re-activate the architectural discipline. Almost as a branding. As if such practice would be the sole way to socially engage and be proactive. This is equally exploited, by many, both in the political and private developing field. When you talked earlier about ghostwriting and whispering into 'policy ears', aiming to influence without claiming authorship, I feel this holds a largely overlooked potential. Also as an educational provocation.

PS
Would you understand in such a perspective the architect as a producer? If you look at the music industry you have producers that are extremely present, putting their unique brand onto something. Though there's also the invisible and immensely impactful kind of producer, clearly operating

out of the spotlight. Producing equals enabling, making something possible, using all the rights, tricks and bits to make sure that it happens. I find this an extremely liberating thought. Maybe every architecture school should offer a course for training as an 'architectural producer'? And then there is of course the pressing question whether you would choose such an option?

LF
It could be very meaningful for a school that claims criticality.

MP
What I like about the idea of a producer in the music industry, is that we are thinking about a shared practice. Maybe the architect gets all too confused with the spotlight artist. The producer is bringing all the pieces together, and that seems a fair comparison for the actual reality of architectural practice.

PS
It is a subject that is fundamentally underexposed in the current architectural discourse. And it's for sure not taught. A producer doesn't rule out any creative aspect, on the contrary. It could be a crucial task ahead.

MS
You can definitely find ways to work in such a demeanor. Though there's still a problem ... If you classify the architect as a producer, you still leave intact the notion of the 'performing artist'. Who is then the artist?

PS
You mean the spotlighted creator?

MS
The artist. This would imply getting rid of the entire notion of a single creator. I don't think it is enough to just say the architect is the producer.

PS
Getting rid of the single creator, that is a serious statement.

THD
Here we have a binary I cannot agree with. It seems perfectly fine that there's an artist somewhere in the process, to help to brand or to narrate the project. As long as there is a part of the productive chain that truly and effectively focuses on serving the public interest. Hence, in this sense the producer could be extremely instrumental.

LS
Perhaps architecture should increasingly become a boring profession. Just as politics, it should be boring, not sexy. It's about a tremendously boring process.

PS
Do you feel boring is the right notion here?

MS
I think we can agree on boring ...

PS
I don't sign up for boring.

LS
Maybe boring is not something bad ...

PS
It reads as passive, the exact opposite of a proactive stance. Voltage free, avoiding any productive conflict ...

LS
It should at least be less visible and not be blindly branded as enticing.

MS
The process should be boring, not the outcome.

PS
If the process is boring, an audience, politics, stakeholders, ..., could react extremely indifferent and lose any sense of engagement or responsibility. Even if you're ghostwriting you should make sure that the process is gripping and problematizing.

THD
So, avoiding becoming a boring producer, or an all too divine one, is the message here!

PS
Indeed.

—

Renoncer, c'est choisir

Although at first it is hard to tell why, I Prefer Not To is a startling sentence. Picture this: I Prefer Not To tell you. I Prefer Not To see you today. I Prefer Not To do this.

Perhaps I Prefer Not To is confusing because it is both blunt and polite. It is carelessly and subtly disruptive in an almost child-like manner. It has the same kind of charming, straightforward vulnerability as Why? or I Don't Know. I Prefer Not To is not mediating, as opposed to other expressions from the neither-yes-or-no spectrum. For example: Yes, But. Yes, But the thing is... Don't you think. Don't you think we should...? I'm Not An Expert But. I'm Not An Expert But I don't think... I'm Sorry But. I Agree But. I Understand But. We'll See. In short, the commonplaces of adult diplomacy.

As opposed to Yes But and co, I Prefer Not To is unsettling because it is unapologetically subjective. It does not foresee any 'rational' or ideological cover. In the case of Herman Melville's character Bartleby, it is striking that he does not give any explanation for why he prefers not to do anything besides what he was strictly hired for. Despite his polite and gentle ways, to the other characters of the novella the scrivener's behavior is incomprehensible, even offensive. They are baffled because Bartleby does not even attempt to justify himself. Above all, they can't believe he gets away with it.

Admittedly, when you are not the one saying it, I Prefer Not To is a pain. Depending on its context it can be interpreted as laziness, caprice, self-complacent heroism, cowardice, bad will, elitism. Someone who only says I Prefer Not To is not only masochistic, but also unbearable. For it to retain its fresh effect, either moderation or consistency are advised.

Perhaps all who hear I Prefer Not To feel affronted because they would rather say it themselves. I Prefer Not To is self-ish; a matter of setting boundaries, of allowing, expressing, preserving a self. In other words, I Prefer Not To is a vital luxury. Rather than must do, should do, can do, there is the deliciously eccentric prefer (not) to do. I Prefer Not To, though lonely, can certainly be pleasurable. And when it is not, at least it is relieving.

The problem is it is hard to predict whether one can afford I Prefer Not To, be it in personal or professional relations. To many I Prefer Not To does not qualify as an option. Perhaps the best definition of being unfree is precisely this: unable to say I Prefer Not To. In other cases, however, it is more about feeling unfree than actually being unfree. Fortunately – or unfortunately – the related reasons tend to be more prosaic: 'responsibilities', contracts, greed, comfort, ambition. Or on an emotional level, the most universally recognizable reason of all: affection.

I Prefer Not To is neither I Won't or You Shouldn't. Strictly speaking, I Prefer Not To does not represent, does not judge, does not propose anything. It is pure, stubborn idiosyncrasy. It is hard to imagine how the individual immobility of I Prefer Not To can signify a change in itself. Yet, I Prefer Not To is never innocent, it is always performative. Even though it is not moralizing, it does bear a clear message. Whether substantiated or not, it is a deliberate choice. At best, I Prefer Not To expresses simultaneously can and can't be bothered; a love-hate relationship.

Beatriz Van Houtte Alonso

Credits

The editor wishes to specifically thank the architects Barbara Campbell-Lange, Philippe Nathan and Mélissa Vrolixs for their decisive insights, critical openness, and boundless generosity.

Biographies

Arno Brandlhuber: (1964, Germany) is founder of the Berlin-based office Brandlhuber+. He studied architecture and urban planning at the Technical University of Darmstadt and the Università degli Studi di Firenze. His cultural practice reaches beyond the limited fields of architecture and urbanism, aiming at politicizing issues of private and collective property, sustainable economy and social cooperation. Seminal projects by Brandlhuber+ are the Berlin Terrassenhause, the Antivilla and the Brunnenstrasse 9 estate. Key exhibitions/publications include *The Property Drama* and *Legislating Architecture*. The office has been awarded numerous national and international prizes including the German Architecture Award. Since 2017 Brandlhuber has been appointed Associate Professor in architectural design at the ETH Zurich.

François Charbonnet: (1972, Switzerland) is co-founder along with Patrick Heiz of the Geneva-based architecture studio Made in. After graduating from the ETH Zurich with a thesis supervised by Prof. Hans Kollhoff, he collaborated with Herzog & de Meuron and OMA, before setting up his own practice in 2003. In addition to his architectural work, he is a frequent lecturer and has been Visiting Professor at the EPF

Lausanne, the Accademia di Architettura, Mendrisio and the Kyoto Design Lab. Since 2018 François Charbonnet has been appointed Professor Architectural Design at the ETH Zurich.

Maarten Delbeke: (1970, Belgium) holds the Chair of the History and Theory of Architecture at the Department of Architecture ETH Zurich. In 2005 he started teaching at the Universities of Ghent and Leiden. In 2014 he became Full Professor in the field of architectural history and theory at Ghent University. Delbeke has published widely on the history and theory of baroque architecture and art, theoretical questions in 18th- and 19th-century European architecture; and the reception of early modern architecture in the 20th century. He is also active as an architecture critic. As the founding editor-in-chief of the online open-access journal 'Architectural Histories', he seeks to explore digital methods in the research and dissemination of architectural history.

Tom Emerson: (1970, France) studied architecture at the University of Bath, the London Royal College of Art and the University of Cambridge. Emerson founded the London based office 6a architects with Stephanie Macdonald in 2001. The practice is best known for its contemporary art galleries, educational buildings, artists' studios and residential projects. 6a architects has received several RIBA Awards, the Schelling Medal (2012) and was shortlisted for the Stirling Prize (2017). Emerson was awarded the Conrad Ferdinand Meyer Prize in Zurich (2018). Work and writings by the practice have been exhibited and published internationally. Tom Emerson taught at the Architectural Association, Cambridge and, since 2010 has been Professor of architecture at the ETH Zurich.

Sophia Holst: (1988, The Netherlands) studied Fine Arts at the Gerrit Rietveld Academy and the Sandberg Intitute in Amsterdam. Later she obtained her architecture degree at the KU Leuven in Brussels. She has worked for Studio Anne Holtrop and NU architectuuratelier and has collaborated with CRIT. Next to that, she is a participant at the postgraduate program of the Jan van Eyck Academy, Maastricht, for 2020-2021. Her Brussels-based practice involves the design as well as the observation of architecture and urban planning through a critical lens of power structures and social paradigms. Her research project 'Forms of Public Privacy' was visible at the FORMAT 2019 exhibition in Z33, Hasselt.

Christian Kerez: (1962, Venezuela) is an architect educated at the Swiss Federal Institute of Technology, ETH

Zurich. After extensive published work in the field of architectural photography, he opened his own architectural office in Zurich, in 1993. He was appointed Visiting Professor at the Swiss Federal Institute of Technology Zurich in 2001, Assistant Professor in 2003 and has been a Full Professor for architectural design since 2009. In 2012, he led the Kenzo Tange Chair at Harvard University Graduate School of Design. For the Swiss Pavilion at the Venice Architecture Biennial 2016 he participated with the acclaimed project 'Incidental Space'. He is currently working on architectural projects at various scales in Germany, Austria, Czech Republic, Bahrain and Dubai.

Anne Lacaton: (1955, France) graduated as an architect in 1980. Together with Jean-Philippe Vassal she co-founded the architectural studio Lacaton & Vassal. Based in Paris, the office exerts an international practice, working on public buildings, housing and urban planning. All projects are based on principles of generosity and economy, working carefully with climate and the existing context. Re-use and transformation are favored over demolition and new constructions. Pivotal works are the Palais de Tokyo (Paris), the Architecture School (Nantes), House Latapie (Bordeaux), Cité Manifeste (Mulhouse) and the transformations of modernist social housing blocks in Paris and Bordeaux.

Luc Tuymans: (1958, Belgium) is considered one of the most significant European painters of his generation. Born and raised in Antwerp, where he lives and works, Luc Tuymans is an inheritor of the vast tradition of Northern European painting. Though, as a child of the 1950s, his relationship to the medium is influenced by photography, television, and cinema. Interested in the effects of World War II, Tuymans explores issues of history and memory, as well as the relationship between photography and painting, using a muted palette to create canvases that are simultaneously withholding and stark. His compositions make use of cropping, close-ups, framing, and sequencing, offering fresh perspectives on the medium of painting, as well as larger cultural issues.

Something Fantastic: (2010, Germany) is an "undisciplinary" architecture practice founded by Leonard Streich, Julian Schubert and Elena Schütz. The firm's agenda is based on the idea that working as architects implies a broad interest and involvement in the world. The studio operates in the extended field of architecture; designing books, exhibitions, furniture, buildings, and urban development schemes. Next to designing, the partners write, teach (ETH Zurich, Sandberg Institute) and art direct (Artek). In 2016 the studio was responsible for the design of the German Pavilion at Venice Architecture Biennial, entitled 'Making Heimat – Germany Arrival Country'. Something Fantastic architectural work has been nominated both for the Iakov Chernikov Prize and the Marcus Prize.

Jan De Vylder: (1968, Belgium) obtained his architecture degree at the Sint-Lucas School of Architecture, Ghent. Together with Inge Vinck and Jo Taillieu, he co-founded architecten de vylder vinck taillieu and more recently architecten jan de vylder inge vinck. Notable projects include the studios for les ballets C de la B & LOD (Ghent), Palais des Expos (Charleroi), and the psychiatric clinic of PC Caritas (Melle) for which the former office, in collaboration with BAVO, received the Silver Lion at the Venice Architecture Biennial (2017). Jan De Vylder has taught at Sint-Lucas School of Architecture (Ghent/Brussels), TU Delft, EPF Lausanne and the Academia di Architettura di Mendrisio. Since 2017, he has been appointed Associate Professor in Architectural Design at the ETH Zurich.

Anri Sala: (1974, Albania) lives and works in Berlin. He studied painting at the Academy of Fine Arts of Tirana and continued his training at the École Nationale Supérieure des Arts Décoratifs in Paris and Le Fresnoy in Tourcoing. Sala's transformative, time-based works investigate ruptures in language, syntax, and music in order to validate or invalidate narrative and composition. Recent exhibitions include solo shows at the French Pavilion of the 55th Venice Art Biennial; Centre Georges Pompidou, Paris; The Serpentine Gallery, London; The Museum of Contemporary Art, North Miami; and the Fondazione Nicola Trussardi, Milan. Sala has received multiple prizes, including the Vincent Award (2014), the 10th Benesse Prize (2013) and the Absolut Art Award (2011).

Laurent Stalder: (1970, Switzerland) studied architecture at the Swiss Federal Institute of Technology, ETH Zurich. Since 2018 he is Full Professor at the gta ETH Zurich, which he heads as well. The main focus of Stalder's research is the history and theory of architecture from the nineteenth to twenty-first century, intersecting with the history of technology. His articles have been published in various journals, including 'AA Files', 'ARCH+', 'The Journal of Architecture'. Laurent Stalder is a member of the (scientific) board of multiple foundations and institutions, including the Werner Oechslin Library Foundation in Einsiedeln, the Swiss Institute for Archaeological and Architectural Research in Cairo, Egypt and the Jaap Bakema Study Centre in Rotterdam.

Peter Swinnen: (1972, Belgium) is a Brussels-based architect merging space production and political policy. After his apprenticeship at Luc Deleu/T.O.P. Office (1996) he co-founded the architectural office 51N4E, which he spearheaded until 2013. From 2010 to 2015 Swinnen enrolled as Flemish State Architect, a public mandate empowering architecture as a policy-making discipline. In 2016 he founded CRIT., a spatial practice addressing modes of architectural policy whispering. Swinnen has taught at the Architectural Association, ETH Zurich, KU Leuven and the University of Luxembourg. He is the recipient of the Maaskant Architecture Award for Young Architects (2004) and the European Prize for Urban Public Space (2018). In 2012, he co-curated 'The Ambition of the Territory' for the Belgian Pavilion at the Venice Architecture Biennial.

Philip Ursprung: (1963, USA) is Professor of History of Art and Architecture at the Department of Architecture at ETH Zurich. From 2017 to 2019 he was Dean of the Department. He earned his PhD in Art History at Freie Universität Berlin after studying in Geneva, Vienna and Berlin. He taught at the Hochschule der Künste Berlin, Columbia University New York, the Barcelona Institute of Architecture and the University of Zurich. He is the editor and author of several books, of which the most recent titles are: 'Brechas y conexiones: Ensayos sobre arquitectura, arte y economia' (2016), 'Der Wert der Oberfläche' (2017) and 'Representation of Labor / Performative Historiography' (2018).

Beatriz Van Houtte Alonso: (1996, Belgium) studied architecture and engineering at the University of Ghent and architectural history at the Bartlett School of Architecture. She is a contributor to De Witte Raaf and researcher at CRIT. architects.

Finn Williams: (1982, UK) is Co-founder and CEO of Public Practice. He previously worked for the Office of Metropolitan Architecture, Croydon Council and the Greater London Authority. Finn has been a member of the Raynsford Review Task Force, Labour Planning Commission, RIBA Planning Group, and the boards of the Planning Officers Society, Planning Advisory Service, and Urban Design London. He is a Visiting Professor of Practice at the Institute of Innovation & Public Purpose at UCL, a Design Council Built Environment Expert, and was co-curator of the British Pavilion at the 2016 Venice Architecture Biennial.

Image credits

In order of appearance:
© Luc Tuymans. © Something Fantastic. © Lacaton & Vassal, images based on lecture by Anne Lacaton (24-05-2017): Maison Latapie, Floirac, France, 1993; Cité manifeste, Mulhouse, France, 2005; Quartier de Grand Parc, block G,H,I, Bordeaux, France, 2016; School of Architecture Nantes, Nantes, France, 2009; 'PLUS - Les grands ensembles de logements - Territoires d'exception', Druot, Lacaton & Vassal, France, 2004. © architecten de vylder vinck taillieu. 'Cell No.2' by Absalon, Wikipedia, image by Tomislav Medak. Fresco of garden Villa di Livia in Rome, 1st century AD. © Studio Tom Emerson / ETH, 'Pavilion of Reflections', Zurich, 2016. © Anri Sala, Film stills from 'Intervista'. Marble sculpture 'Truth Unveiled by Time' by Gian Lorenzo Bernini, Rome, 1652, Wikipedia, image by Paolo Monti. All spreads taken from lecture by Finn Williams (28-11-2017), for sources see lecture. All images taken from lecture by Arno Brandlhuber (8-11-2016), for sources see lecture. Students during discussion, Studio Swinnen, surrounding ETH Zurich, 2017, Images by: Philippe Nathan / ETH Studio Swinnen.

Colophon

Editor: Peter Swinnen

Form: Something Fantastic A.D.
with Fernanda Tellez Velasco

Assistants to the Editor:
Sophia Holst, Tom Schoonjans
and Beatriz Van Houtte Alonso

Proofreader: Anne Judong

Lithogaphy: Falk Flach

Print: C.H. Beck

Paper: Lux Cream, Peydur
Feinleinen

Fonts: Life, Arial

Published by Verlag der
Buchhandlung Walther und
Franz König
Ehrenstraße 4, D-50672 Köln

Bibliographic information
published by the Deutsche
Nationalbibliothek
The Deutsche Nationalbibliothek
lists this publication in the
Deutsche Nationalbibliografie;
detailed bibliographic data are
available in the Internet at
http://dnb.d-nb.de.

Printed in Germany

Distribution Europe:
Buchhandlung Walther König
Ehrenstraße 4,
D - 50672 Köln
Tel: +49 (0) 221 / 20 59 6 53
verlag@buchhandlung-walther
-koenig.de

Distribution UK & Ireland:
Cornerhouse Publications
Ltd. - HOME
2 Tony Wilson Place
UK – Manchester M15 4FN
Tel: +44 (0) 161 212 3466
publications@cornerhouse.org

Distribution Outside Europe:
D.A.P. / Distributed Art
Publishers, Inc.
75 Broad Street, Suite 630
USA - New York, NY 10004
Tel: +1 (0) 212 627 1999
orders@dapinc.com

ISBN 978-3-7533-0135-8